PRAISE FOR *JOY AND SUCCESS AT WORK*

"Mark has captured the essence of what I strive for as a leader—shepherding a strong business, innovating great products that customers love, and, most importantly, inspiring a value-driven culture where employees bring their whole selves to work every day. We spend more of our discretionary time with our work family than our personal families; this book demonstrates how to create an environment where joy and success are possible at work."

–Pat Gelsinger

CEO, VMWare

"The road to success is a lot easier if you can travel with someone who's navigated that road and developed a map. In *Joy and Success at Work*, Mark McClain shares the wisdom he has gained over a lifetime of business success in a fun and engaging way. In it, he gives people who want to experience the broadest definition of success a lot to work with."

–Stephen Quinn

former executive vice president and chief marketing officer, Walmart Stores

"Mark McClain has a genuine concern for young organizations and leaders 'getting it right.' Few authors speak to the essentials in such a credible, authentic, easy-to-read, and 'easy-to-get' format. This is a 'must-read.'"

–Mark W. Albers

senior vice president (retired), ExxonMobil

"Great leaders understand the importance of culture—it eats strategy for lunch! In his new book, Mark reveals the requisite ingredients needed to create a values-based culture, which underpins great products and satisfied customers while allowing everyone in the process to have fun. I know Mark personally and highly respect him as a competent business leader, husband, father, and man of faith. Anyone who is serious about creating an environment that leads to both joy and success at work will take the time to read this easy-to-digest book."

—Dr. Rick Lytle

president and CEO, The CEO Forum

"If you are searching for a market-leading ROI from investments targeting your personal or company leadership development, read and absorb this book! McClain conveys unconventional wisdom served up in bite-size chapters that entertain as well as inform. Valuable, engaging read that's relevant!"

—Carlos Sepulveda

chairman of TBK Bank; lead director of Cinemark Board; and former CEO and president of Interstate Batteries

"Mark didn't need to write a book, but I'm glad he did. The world needs more leaders leading like Mark, and the witty, practical, and portable insights he shares can help any leader help any organization be better!"

—Mike Sharrow

CEO, The C12 Group

"No one who knows Mark will be surprised that he wrote this book. Neither will they be surprised at how well he successfully distills in *Joy and Success at Work* the most fundamental tenets of how to achieve organizational success through employees who love what they do. Mark has always 'walked the talk' and *Joy and Success at Work* does an exceptional job of sharing his powerful management philosophy in an on-demand, easily accessible format."

—Bill Wood

general partner, Bill Wood Ventures

"I've had the chance to get to know Mark as Jeff and I have been on our own entrepreneurial journey at Camp Gladiator, and I'm so excited to see him capture the essence of his philosophy about building a successful business and creating a joyful environment while doing it! We've learned a lot as we've talked to Mark about some of our own challenges growing a successful business based on core values, and we are so glad that this book will give you the opportunity to learn from these principles as well!"

—Ally Davidson

founder and Co-CEO, Camp Gladiator

"This is a must-read for anyone who desires to experience a sustainable 'wholistic' approach to life, leadership, the love of labor, and people. Mark has given us more than 'take it or leave it' advice. He has given us wisdom from experience that should be acted upon."

—Steve Menefee

president for North America and Asia Pacific (retired), Arrow Electronics

"Mark McClain provides a guide to building value but not only of the financial nature. He focuses on the innovative value of product that fits a market and the holistic value of the people who deliver it. Mark understands that culture drives organizational performance and that values drive culture. High standards, strong ethics, a commitment to people, and a passion to do the right thing—these contribute to an organizational culture that can achieve greatness, with fun along the way. It is possible to have both joy *and* success."

—Bill Bock
chairman of the board, SailPoint

"I worked with Mark as an early investor in both of his start-up companies. I've seen how his team's approach to building market-driven products in the context of a values-based culture was a great formula for success. If you're working on your own entrepreneurial venture, I highly recommend you pick up this book and refer to it often."

—Ravi Mhatre
general partner, Lightspeed Venture Partners

"In a sea of books on business leadership, Mark McClain has produced a gem, and made a valuable contribution to the field. It matters not what your position on the org chart or the tax bracket your current job places you, if you hate what you do. Life is too important, and too brief, to spend it joylessly. Packed with wisdom, this book will direct you to the path that leads not only to success in business, but success in life."

—Dr. Richard Blackaby
president, Blackaby Ministries International; author of Spiritual Leadership

"I've known Mark for almost twenty-five years, and he practices what he preaches. He has built multiple successful businesses, based on the core values we both share. What's fun to watch is how Mark does this while treating people according to the Golden Rule, which has enabled him to bring real joy into the lives of the people who work with him. I recommend this book for leaders in any setting who are committed to balancing joy *and* success at work."

—Dr. Matt Cassidy

senior pastor, Grace Covenant Church

"Mark is one of my favorite faith-driven entrepreneurs of all time. He's out there making it happen, innovating, creating, slaying dragons, and loving on people all while being intentional about 'why' he does what he does."

—Henry Kaestner

cofounder, faith-driven entrepreneur, and former CEO and chairman, Bandwidth

"Upon encountering Mark McClain, face-to-face or in written form, what you see is what you get—an energetic and gregarious Christ-follower who dearly loves his family, treasures his colleagues and friends, and is an exceptional community leader *who just happens* to be CEO of SailPoint. In other words, Mark leads a big life. His professional success is enviable, but there are other things considerably more meaningful and valuable to him. While business schools understandably focus on leveraging intelligence to produce competent business leaders, Mark beautifully demonstrates how competency *and* bringing one's whole self into the C-suite—asking oneself 'how will I love my people today?'—can create a culture that generates strong competitive advantage. Mark's generosity, exceptional wit, and infectious sense of humor are clearly present here, as are his authenticity, humility, and desire to help others in their professional journeys. This book is long overdue!"

—Tony Budet

president and CEO, University Federal Credit Union

JOY *and* SUCCESS

SUCCESS

AT WORK

JOY *and* OR SUCCESS

AT WORK

BUILDING ORGANIZATIONS THAT DON'T SUCK

the life out of people.

MARK McCLAIN

ForbesBooks

Published by ForbesBooks, Charleston, South Carolina.
Member of Advantage Media Group.

ForbesBooks is a registered trademark, and the ForbesBooks colophon is a trademark of Forbes Media, LLC.

Printed in the United States of America.

10 9 8 7 6 5 4 3 2 1

ISBN: 978-1-95086-304-4
LCCN: 2019918698

Cover and layout design by George Stevens.

This publication is designed to provide accurate and authoritative information in regard to the subject matter covered. It is sold with the understanding that the publisher is not engaged in rendering legal, accounting, or other professional services. If legal advice or other expert assistance is required, the services of a competent professional person should be sought.

Advantage Media Group is proud to be a part of the Tree Neutral® program. Tree Neutral offsets the number of trees consumed in the production and printing of this book by taking proactive steps such as planting trees in direct proportion to the number of trees used to print books. To learn more about Tree Neutral, please visit **www.treeneutral.com**.

Since 1917, the Forbes mission has remained constant. Global Champions of Entrepreneurial Capitalism. ForbesBooks exists to further that aim by bringing the Stories, Passion, and Knowledge of top thought leaders to the forefront. ForbesBooks brings you The Best in Business. To be considered for publication, please visit **www.forbesbooks.com**.

To Marj—because you have been with me on this entire journey, it has been both a great adventure and a great joy. I love you forever.

ACKNOWLEDGMENTS

This book is the result of trying to distill about thirty-five years of experience in the world of work. As you might expect, it is simply impossible to thank all those who have helped me along this journey. However, I am particularly indebted to my family, without whose love and understanding I would never have been able to find a way to have a ridiculously joyful existence and still manage to do some interesting things in the marketplace. I also owe a great debt of gratitude to my cofounders across Waveset and SailPoint—Kevin (twice!), Mike, Bill, and Jackie—whose friendship, support, and unbelievable talent have marked my last twenty-five years indelibly. I have enjoyed the opportunity to work with amazing friends and colleagues over the years, particularly Matt, Ray, Dan, Andy, Cam, a number of Daves, and the rest of our core team at SailPoint. It is because of these hundreds and hundreds of people that I have been able to enjoy whatever success has come in the world of work. Lastly and most importantly, I am grateful to God for giving me life and breath each moment. It is for His Glory that I do everything.

A WORD FROM THE AUTHOR

(Skip This at Your Peril!)

MANY THOUSANDS OF BOOKS have already been written on management and leadership. I've found several inspiring.

I love everything Patrick Lencioni has written. I think Geoffrey Moore is amazing. Blanchard and Johnson's *The One Minute Manager* should be required reading for anyone in a leadership role. Many others have influenced me, too many to list here—but I've called them out in the main text (and on the resources page).

While all these thinkers on management and leadership have influenced and inspired me, I've often come away from many books on leadership feeling they lacked an element I find crucial to success in any endeavor: *joy.*

Is that because injecting humor into a treatise on leadership would prevent it from being taken seriously? I don't know. But I do know this: I *didn't* want to write a *treatise.*

I wanted to create a *manual,* a guide for leaders and managers seeking help *right now,* in which they could quickly find the answers they needed and hopefully a laugh or two along the way. Its topics would be clear and easy to locate. After all, who has the time or patience to sift through long chapters to find what they need, especially in an age when information is a click away?

So I knew what I wanted and (just as important—and always true) what I *didn't* want. But how to create it?

I was stunned to learn that someone already had, masterfully, *fifty years* ago in a book that had been recommended to me often: *Up the Organization* by Robert Townsend.

Townsend, who died in 1998, gained fame for leading Avis, the car-rental giant, from money-bleeding mediocrity to profitable excellence, largely on the strength of one of the most iconic advertising slogans of all time: "When you're only No. 2, you try harder. Or else."

Before joining Avis, Townsend led American Express. His primary tools were an often-brutal honesty; an irreverent sense of humor; and an energy and enthusiasm that even his editor, Robert Gottlieb at Knopf, admitted in his homage to Townsend for the thirty-fifth anniversary edition of *Up the Organization*: "Could be wearing at times." Yet Gottlieb quickly added, "From the creative point of view, he was absolutely brilliant."

Up the Organization became a best seller. Many still rank it among the best management books of all time. In it, Townsend shares, often hilariously, techniques he applied in turning around organizations that had become too big and/or too set in their ways for their own good.

Now let me be clear: I'm *not* Robert Townsend. Nor is this book meant to duplicate (or hold a candle to) *Up the Organization*. There will never be another. It's that good.

But I'm also not above borrowing Townsend's structure. It, too, is that good.

Beyond its ease of use, something else about *Up the Organization* spoke to me. I realized that, like Townsend, I've spent most of my life creating and leading organizations based on a management theory I never knew existed. It's called *Theory Y*, and it puts *people* first.

And while Theory Y leadership largely enabled Townsend's approaches for turning *legacy* companies around, it's also how I believe he would have created *new* companies if, like me, he'd been of the entrepreneurial persuasion.

Since Townsend is no longer with us, we'll never know for sure. But this I can say without equivocation: where *Up the Organization* took an unflinching look at how *existing* companies get well, I've done my level best to convey, without compromise, a sound approach to—and the potential pitfalls in—building and leading newer ones.

Up the Organization helped me see that what is missing in too many start-ups and growing companies today is the same thing Townsend saw lacking in the already-existing organizations he fixed: a no-nonsense, people-centered approach. And though our ideologies align, to his central tenet of "getting there isn't half the fun; it's all the fun," I would add that having fun is impossible if you don't *hire and retain the right people.*

That conviction has played a huge role in my approach to leadership and speaks directly to the attributes I think matter most: humility, transparency, and genuine concern for every person our companies touch. These qualities are natural by-products of work cultures that *encourage employee initiative and innovation.* Which, I've since learned, is pretty much the foundation of Theory Y leadership.

But this is no psychology book. It shares my experiences in founding and leading such organizations—warts and all. By doing so, I hope to help a *new* generation of leaders discover a fundamental truth, just as I have and as Townsend did before me: when *each* of us is committed to helping *one another* succeed in *every* facet of life, we not only find success but have great fun while we're at it.

WHO I AM, AND HOW I CAN HELP

Since I'm a first-time author, the thought of writing a book was a little scary.

There was the time commitment, of course. I'm the founder and CEO of a publicly traded company. That alone probably should have convinced me that I had more pressing things to do. (Shhhh … don't tell the shareholders!)

There's also the fact that committing thousands of words to paper required no small amount of faith that I could do so in a way that makes people *actually want to read them*. I'd not only have to immediately *engage* readers but *continue* doing so, page after page, in an authoritative, complete, and ultimately *compelling* way.

That last thing was scariest of all: Could my words, however eloquent (or not?), really prompt other leaders to *act*? To decide that the information and ideas shared are important enough that their organizations would be *markedly better* for having implemented them?

One thing counterbalanced these fears and tipped the scale in favor of giving it a shot: my work mentoring younger entrepreneurs here in Austin. It is work I truly love.

In doing it—and thanks to a lifetime of founding and observing and learning about and leading great, profitable companies—I've become all too familiar with the ill effects of what I call pseudocultures: thinly veiled come-ons (chefs, massages, free beer, whatever) that new companies use to attract employees and (try) to impress potential investors and customers.

Some inevitably buy in, but before long (and often, the hard way) they figure it out: a couple of interesting ideas and a cool employee lounge with beanbag chairs and a ping-pong table do not a successful company make.

Real organizational cultures are reflections of how companies treat people and *actually do* things, like create useful products.

Real *leaders* are therefore most interested in market and product issues. *And* customer and employee issues. *And* investor, and legal, and tax, and a whole host of *other* issues. They also understand that sustainable company cultures grow out of innovation—not the other way around.

If it were possible to create great products by building a gym and paying workers to go play in it, everybody'd be doing it. The fact that such efforts inevitably fail should tell would-be leaders all they need to know. But sadly, lots of otherwise smart people continue trying to start companies by creating culture first and believing—instead of confirming—that their ideas will attain marketability (i.e., become products). Conversely, leaders who understand the importance of offering customers a product they desperately need but which is not yet available know that *ideas alone* have no market value.

Maybe this is why Jobs and Wozniak were not outside the garage playing basketball but inside playing with (and thinking and talking about, and eating, and sleeping, and breathing) the rudiments of what would become their world-changing products at Apple.

This book aims to help leaders and managers of new and growing companies avoid pitfalls like pseudocultures and half-baked products—and thereby, to *also* avoid self-destruction. It shares my experience across more than twenty years of founding, scaling, and leading several companies, including one I cofounded in 2004 and now serve as CEO: SailPoint Technologies.

Most of what I share is drawn from my work at SailPoint because it has been my most successful (and longest-term) venture. Many years of trial, error, failure, and (finally) success preceded it. I neither gloss over nor try to embellish those experiences here. They were formative and, as such, informed the approaches I applied in leading SailPoint from an idea through venture capital and private equity backing to an IPO.

Now we're an approximately $2 billion market-cap company with 1,200 employees. My greatest point of pride is our achievement of that growth and success *while maintaining* one of Glassdoor's highest ratings for company culture and CEO approval. In our rate-everything-instantly world, that is no mean feat, and we did it mainly by spurning the pseudoculture and idea-as-product ethos—which, even now, is running rampant in the start-up and venture capital world.

I can't say when that shift occurred, probably because it happened so gradually. But this much I know: incubating a company should not resemble a Hollywood pitch meeting, with people throwing around ideas and picking whatever sounds likely to have a killer opening weekend.

As leaders, we must bury, once and for all, the notion that companies can make people happy by offering pseudo or half-baked *anything*—and that it's okay to treat people like something other than humans. Until we do, firms will keep chasing the wrong rabbits down the wrong holes and wasting human capital that could be spent far more wisely.

Lasting success requires a genuine commitment to *mutual* success—of customers, employees, investors, *and* the company itself.

With this book, I invite you to join me in that pursuit, and I offer proven techniques for getting there.

Like Robert Townsend's classic (a book I urge you to read, by the way … *after* this one!) the table of contents is also an index, so it's easy to use this book as a manual. You can quickly find what you're looking for, turn to it, and (quoting Townsend) "read all I have to say about it in five minutes or less."

MARK McCLAIN

Austin, Texas

January 2020

CONTENTS

N

O

P

R

AUTHENTICITY

IT'S NICE TO THINK that things are always great, and far be it from me to espouse anything but a positive attitude. I sincerely believe it makes a big difference in life in a lot of fundamental ways.

There are risks, however, in putting a positive spin on things all the time—notably, it can affect whether your stakeholders, in particular your team members, see you, the company's leader, as authentic.

For me, one test of authenticity is a willingness to acknowledge when things aren't that great or even when they're really bad. I was joking about this in a talk I gave recently, how some people are all about transparency and authenticity—provided things are going well. They are positive, literally, to a fault, because when things are not going great, they get quiet, duck hallway conversations, and walk around the office with their heads down.

Soon people get the *one thought* in their heads that freezes up workplaces like no other: "What's wrong?"

You can't be authentic and offer only happy talk. You have to provide the good news and the bad. In short, you have to treat your people like adults. Ultimately, it comes down to trust. When you really trust people, you tell them as much as you can about how

You can't be authentic and offer only happy talk. You have to provide the good news and the bad.

things are actually going.

Maybe the last quarter was tough. How you communicate that in a prepublic versus postpublic company will differ, not least because in a public company, everybody who's not an insider has to hear it at the same time. An advantage of a private company is the ability to be pretty open about how things are going in real time, unconcerned with the effect it may have on your share price.

As you transition to a public setting, sometimes you have to keep certain information (like earnings) under wraps till you're ready to share it with everyone at once. But the goal is still the same: be authentic, speak the truth, and treat people like adults.

AWARENESS, SELF-

MUCH ABOUT THE BUSINESS world is challenging. But almost without exception, I have found that people who are not doing as well as they could be in their jobs tend to be suffering from a relatively easy-to-address problem: a lack of self-awareness.

Specifically, the person's view of their own skills and abilities is not in tune with reality.

People do their best work when they are clear on what they're good at—and, just as important, what they're *not* so good at.

Unfortunately, many companies actually contribute to, if not downright *create*, their struggling employees' lack of self-awareness through a ritual that is *de rigueur* at most organizations: the performance review.

> *People do their best work when they are clear on what they're good at—and, just as important, what they're* not *so good at.*

An employee sits down in her boss's office and is told, "Here's what you're doing well, and here's what you're not doing well." Often, she is given examples of both.

5

The praise is nice, but human nature ensures that hearing about one's shortcomings really stings. Then her boss encourages her to focus her time and energy on fixing them.

And so she does, even though the areas in which she is found lacking are things that, although potentially useful, could easily be handled by others while she could (and should) stay focused on leveraging her strengths.

It all happens in the name of "employee development."

Somewhere along the line, some managers began to embrace the notion that *all* their people should be good at everything—or at least, at as much as possible. Which is nonsense. It is also why the Peter Principle exists. (In case you've forgotten or are unfamiliar, it states that people in a hierarchy tend to rise to their level of incompetence.)

In fact, a very small percentage of employees wants to spend a lot of time striving to get good at things at which they're not naturally gifted. It's why not everyone works on their own car, why pro tennis players don't also play soccer, and why most software developers aren't typically interested in selling stuff.

So why would we ask employees to get more comfortable—let alone excel—at things *they* are not interested in and weren't hired to do?

Don Clifton, the late chairman of Gallup, brilliantly proved the power of freeing people to do what they love with his CliftonStrengths assessment. His work was recognized by the American Psychological Association, which called him "the father of strengths-based psychology and the grandfather of positive psychology." (You can learn more about and take the assessment at gallupstrengthcenter.com.)

But I digress. I promised in the foreword that this is not a psychology book.

What matters most about self-awareness is this: the things people do best are the things they love doing, or at minimum, that they care enough about that they might learn to love doing them. When you free all your people to do what they love (or think they might love) instead of requiring them to learn and do things they don't love, you not only strengthen their self-awareness but take a big step toward making your company more effective, efficient, and profitable.

So stop trying to turn accountants into salespeople and everyone into managers. Hire accountants, and let them do their jobs. Hire salespeople, and let them do theirs. Same for engineers, production people—everyone. Then wait for *them* to ask for greater challenges. And for crying out loud, do NOT promote people into management just because they are good at their functions (*see* "Manager—or Not?").

BALANCE, LIFE-WORK

THE DESIRE (AND NECESSITY) of living a balanced life is, at this point, an inescapable topic. And not just at work.

At home, on vacation, out for a hike, and within every community in which we, ummm, commune—friends and relatives, the neighborhood, with gym or yoga buddies, in our churches and spiritual groups—it is increasingly common to talk about how balanced our lives are.

Or that we wish they were.

Thirty or fifty years ago, talking about such stuff, especially at work, was more likely to get you labeled "soft" than "healthy," and nobody's happier than me that those days are gone.

If you've read the first chapter, "Authenticity," you probably know why I've flipped the usual order of this elusive balance from "work-life" to "life-work." We've all heard some variation of "your job is what you do, not who you are." At SailPoint, we back that up. If wherever you are working on at the moment doesn't, it's a safe bet that what keeps you there are life circumstances that necessitate tolerating it—at least for now. You've opted for something I'll discuss in more detail in a moment: a temporary, healthy *im*balance.

Something else that would get you in trouble thirty and more years ago—still can—is talking about faith at work with the aim of converting people: proselytizing. I'm a committed Christian, and while you may or may not be reading this at work, rest assured: this is not a proselytizing book.

Still, if you're serious about finding life-work balance, there's broad agreement that it's essential to consider your spiritual and emotional health.

Some spiritual people will say, "God first, then family, then work." Then golf (or skiing, or kayaking or collecting Atari video games ... or whatever). My point is it's a rank-ordered list. And I've come to believe that's just not the best way to think about it.

Try instead a pie chart, where each "slice of life" is assigned a "perfect" percentage. Maybe yours looks like this:

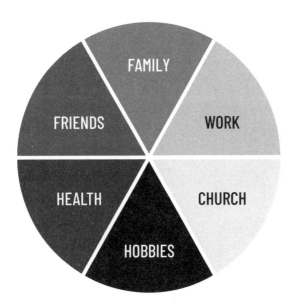

You'll notice that each slice—work, family, friends, health, hobbies, and church—takes up exactly one-sixth of the chart.

Whatever your chart looks like, the next natural thing is to think, "All righty! Now I'll just get all these slices right where I want them, and *voila!* I've balanced my life!"

Not so fast, professor.

Life circumstances change day by day—sometimes hour by hour.

I was talking about this one day with my buddy Matt Cassidy, who happens to be a pastor (*still not proselytizing!*). In the end, we came up with this thought:

A balanced life is one in which we are able to recognize and successfully navigate *temporary healthy imbalances.*

And what exactly are *those?*

Say, as I suggested several paragraphs before, you're working at a place that behaves as if what you do is who you are. I noted that it's likely life circumstances are forcing you to tolerate it—for now.

As in, temporarily.

But hopefully, you're working there only because it's your best option—*for now.*

In other words: it's *healthy.* Not ideal, but it beats the heck out of earning a lot less somewhere else and maybe having to work a second job.

Plus, toughing it out—again, for now—is likely to open doors. You're learning about other players in the industry. Or that you don't want to be in this *piece* of the industry. Or *in this industry at all.* But just by going in to work each day, even though your life's slices are not in the proportions you envision, you are saying, "Tolerating this *imbalance* for now is my best option."

And there you have it: Temporary. Healthy. Imbalance.

(Hey, Matt and I never claimed it was *catchy!*)

Getting that picture of your total pie in your head (putting it

A balanced life is one in which we are able to recognize and successfully navigate temporary healthy imbalances.

on paper really helps) helps you quickly realize that you're always a *little* out of balance (at least). Also that the moments when you feel in *perfect* balance are fleeting—if not downright illusory. Still, when you get close, you'll instantly know it.

You'll also know when things start to feel *more* than a little out of balance.

That's the time to ask yourself, "Can I manage this imbalance for a period of time and then get back closer to my vision of balance? Can I *realistically* make this a *temporary* healthy imbalance?"

If your answer's "no"—if you sense the imbalance will become *permanent*—you don't want to go down that road.

Let's say, for example, that your spouse or child gets sick. The slice of pie labeled "family" grows. You're in a caregiving role at home, so work and other slices of your life pie shrink. And even though you're not the one with the health issue, your health could suffer if their illness becomes serious or chronic—increasing the size of the "family" slice even more.

Or let's think about the "work" slice.

Have you ever said to yourself, "I'm going to have to work a little harder because I'm in a crunch period." Of course. Who hasn't? Whatever kind of work you do, there will be times that pretty much *demand* an out-of-balance segment—a level of intensity that builds like a wave, then breaks and then recedes.

In tech, it can be a new software delivery cycle. For lawyers, it might be prepping their closing argument. For writers, it's being on deadline.

The *trick* is *consciously* cycling back after the wave breaks. *Reasserting* balance, so the slices of your life are closer to where you've pictured them.

If instead you allow yourself to establish a "new normal" of working seventy hours a week and stay there, the "life" side of life-work balance is going to suffer. And you are too.

All of this seems obvious enough when we read it in a book, but life isn't like reading a book. It happens moment by moment, and in trying to make sense of it, we too often resort to those darned rank-ordered lists and focus on whatever we've deemed number one. We attend to that thing first and just *hope* the rest will take care of itself.

I have news for you: it won't.

I learned long ago that if my family has a crisis, *that's* my priority. Period. I will drop work for my family, no questions asked. I never wanted to be some really successful business guy who's onto his fourth or fifth marriage and has adult kids in rehab but lives in a *beautiful* home—all by himself. Does anyone?

Yet it can happen more easily than people think. Here's why.

Imagine two lines that start close together and run parallel. If you change the angle of one line so it's headed just one degree away from the other, the lines, over a short distance, won't drift far apart. But over the course of a mile, or many miles, the divergence becomes bigger—and keeps growing.

Imagine these are not lines in space but *time* lines—one representing your life, the other your work.

And that is how gradually—almost imperceptibly—a "temporary" healthy imbalance, undetected (or left uncorrected), becomes permanent and unhealthy.

I know. It nearly happened to me.

I must preface this—because I really hate sleeping on the couch—by saying that my wife, Marj, is arguably among the top ten partners not only in the history of marriage but in any endeavor, worldwide, since the beginning of time. Without her, I simply would not be half the man I am today. The story that follows is a case example of why.

We'd been married maybe ten years, and one day, she confronted me about the time I was devoting to work. She'd mentioned it once or twice before, and I replied this time as I always had: "I'm just kind of in this cycle," I said. "It will be temporary."

As before, I used the wave analogy: "After this wave breaks, there'll be a down cycle, and things will get back to normal."

This time, it didn't work.

"You know, honey," Marj began, "that's the thing. There *haven't been* any down cycles lately. It just sort of goes from this wave to the next wave to the next wave. I feel like we've established a new baseline—of *too much*."

She'd put her finger *right* on it: my temporary healthy imbalance had become permanently unhealthy. And *until that moment*, I hadn't even realized I'd crossed the line.

After that, my life pie looked a bit different than the one illustrated earlier:

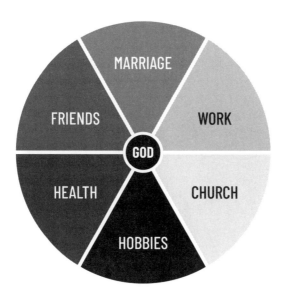

We can't be truly whole if we're alone. We need help. We need grounding.

Taking care of our own well-being is not selfish; it is how we free ourselves to fully engage in the other segments of life.

For me, that derives from spiritual health. As a Christian, it's best exemplified for me in Jesus's response to being asked, "What is the greatest commandment?"

His reply, "To love God and then love others as yourself," completely captures the way I try to lead my life and my company. Keeping God at the center of my life keeps me spiritually healthy.

Others may take comfort and strength from knowing they are emotionally and mentally whole. Maybe you get that from meditation. Or yoga. Or a walk in the woods. But whatever does it for you and however you describe it, at bottom, it means the same thing: *taking care of yourself*. Grounding yourself.

Any psychologist will tell you that it's impossible to love the others in your life well if you don't love yourself well. They're not advocating an unhealthy, narcissistic kind of self-love but a *self-respecting* one. Caring enough about your own well-being that you put it at the center of your life, because that's how you get the spiritual (or emotional, or mental, or self-respecting) aspect of your life right. Today, my chart looks like this:

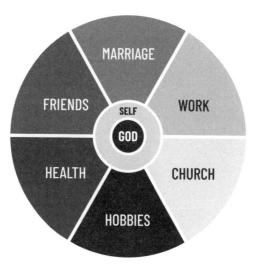

Taking care of our own well-being is not selfish; it is how we free ourselves to fully engage in the *other* segments of life. It keeps us finely attuned to and able to quickly spot wrinkles in life-work balance.

That knowledge opens the door to accepting—or avoiding— bigger imbalances based on their likelihood of being temporary and healthy or more lasting and unhealthy. But early recognition of the imbalance is the key. Miss it, and falling into a permanent unhealthy imbalance becomes a lot more likely.

YOUR MONEY—*AND* YOUR LIFE

I want to give you one last angle on this.

When you sit with a wealth manager, they will allocate your investments, balancing them based on your goals and risk tolerance. They'll put x percent in, say, fixed income securities, y in domestic and/or international stocks, z in large cap, or in small cap, or in bonds, maybe.

Whatever the allocations, though, they will make sure the market sectors and investment types are diverse enough to allow for *rebalancing to your benefit* as market conditions change and as you progress through life and exhibit different tolerances for risk and return. That allows the wealth manager to leverage changing market conditions to produce the returns you want over the long term.

That's what I'm advocating here: a *conscious effort* to balance and rebalance as conditions change to maximize your return—*on life*.

To do that, you need that ideal in mind, that target you can focus on but not get stressed about not hitting. You need to accept that you'll kind of *pass through it* on your way to the *next* temporary healthy imbalance, but that as you do, you'll get this sense of, "Oh, wow. That felt really great there for a little bit." The more that happens, the closer you'll get to the ideal.

You might never reach a permanent *perfect* balance. Indeed, you probably won't: life circumstances are just too dynamic. But with a clear picture in mind, we can get increasingly—and over the long term, extremely—close.

BALANCE, OUT OF

ONE CHALLENGE LEADERS AND managers routinely face is to recognize when the people around them—peers, colleagues, but especially subordinates—are out of balance or are heading in that direction. Beyond the potential impacts on *their* personal lives, you want to try to head off the negative effects such imbalances can have on their roles in the company.

This may seem imposing, but if you're paying attention, this is a red flag that is pretty hard to miss, because it nearly always manifests itself in one of two ways: being at work too much or almost never. Of the two, the first is harder to spot—because what manager doesn't adore a dedicated worker, right?

No one can run at a crazy pace forever. You just can't sustain it. But how do you broach the subject? This usually works for me:

"You're twenty-four [or whatever], and I get it: you think you can sprint a marathon. But I'm fifty-seven, and I know you can't!"

Unfortunately, there's a mind-set in the leadership of certain industries—maybe in the industry from whence this subject worker came—that you *actually let people do that*! You let them burn out, or quit, or (in the most extreme cases) *die*—because you can always replace them, always find another cog to make the wheel turn.

One highly competitive industry (which I won't call out by name) is notorious for this. It hires kids right out of college and works them like dogs for a few years. Those who can't stand it get out, and the HR departments *plan* on the fact that in four to five years, only 15 to 20 percent of those young people will be able to hang in and start moving up the ranks toward senior manager, partner, or whatever. That's their actual, working, do-it-every-day model!

And it's just wrong. We're better than that, aren't we?

There are always going to be ultramotivated climbers, and I'm not saying that in itself that's a bad thing. (Well, it usually is. *See* "Balance, Life-Work.") But exploiting it—to the detriment of the vast majority of your hires—that's beyond bad. It's also the worst kind of laziness.

These types of organizations could choose instead to invest in prehiring assessments to screen out—and thereby save—those who value a life outside work. Doing so would save the companies time and money and turnover and net them more of the people they want right out of the gate. That their profit motives are too great to allow them to see that forest for the trees is beyond disturbing.

At SailPoint, we have a cultural commitment to saying, "Look. In our company, that's not the way it works. We're going to expect a lot of you, but we don't want you to fry yourself, or screw up your health, or screw up your young family if you have one, or your relationships, or whatever. Not only because of what it's going to do to you but because of what it's going to do to us, too, in the long run."

If you have good people, ideally you'd grow them and keep them and help them work toward their vision of a healthy life-work balance.

If we really believe in that, our job as leaders is to be on the lookout for both extremes: working too much and coasting by. Because we'll see both, the sooner we confront it, the more meat we put on the bones of company culture.

Spotting these extremes is easy. What's tougher is spotting folks who are not fully engaged.

It's a gut feeling that is only developed over time, but fortunately, it is easy to develop. All it takes is the determination to know your people—as individuals. Not all managers are willing to do that. To which, much as I hate to, I must suggest that they are probably not management material.

Like it or not, being a counselor of sorts is part of managing people. Because they *are* people. Getting to know them as people, and their work styles, is what makes spotting imbalances possible. It's why good managers pull employees aside and say, "Hey, you're here, but you're not engaged. Is something going on?"

You can't invade their privacy, but you can show concern— and it's no coincidence that managers who do are able to uncover a marriage in trouble, financial issues, alcohol or substance abuse, or any of a host of other issues—and steer their employees to the help they need.

That help is becoming increasingly easy to find. At SailPoint, we've implemented workplace and marketplace chaplains, and we're not alone—it's a growing trend in workplaces, and surprisingly, the engagements they have with people are not necessarily or even often about faith. It's about having somebody who can help you work through tough times. Many companies have taken these employee assistance programs off site to a third party that employees can contact by phone.

I'm not 100 percent sold on that approach, because in my experience it's not going to offer the level of help that most people in

If you have good people, ideally you'd grow them and keep them and help them work toward their vision of a healthy life-work balance.

crisis need. But neither am I opposed to it, because in cases in which people just need to open up and talk to someone, it might be perfect.

At SailPoint, we implemented our chaplaincies with a very light touch, with part-time folks who pop in and out, and while everything is confidential in terms of who is seeing them, I do get a broad report that groups the issues by type. The most common are aging parent and—go figure!—teenager issues. So not necessarily spiritual or health concerns, but the chaplains who serve our company are equipped to handle anything and to refer the employee to other resources if they might help. And most important in terms of the company is that the person has taken action to address the issue, whatever it may be, so they can be fully engaged while at work.

My last thought on this idea of spotting and helping out-of-balance employees is simple: we can talk about caring for our coworkers until we're blue in the face. But when we get to know them and put in place the pieces that help them succeed, we walk the talk—and everybody wins.

BOARDS, WORKING WITH

I'VE WORKED WITH THREE different boards of directors, one each of three types. Knowing the general principles that apply across them all—universal truths, so to speak—is a good place to begin any discussion about working with a board. Later, I'll get into some specifics about each type: venture capital (VC), private equity (PE), and public company boards.

IN GENERAL

A few things are nearly always true when you're working with a board, and right at the top is deciding whether you need one in the first place. All my start-ups have been investor backed, but when you don't go that route, you may be tempted not to have a board at all.

Big mistake.

Young companies need all the perspective they can get. A *sounding* board, composed of people with an interest in your venture's

The quickest way to relinquish the mantle of leadership is by planting seeds of doubt within your board about whether you are the best person to wear it.

success, provides it. So universal truth number one: *Every company can benefit from a having a board.*

Universal truth number two: *Use your board for its intended purpose: providing advice and perspective.*

Never bring a problem to your board if you don't want their help in solving it, because they *will* want to help—at least. At worst, one or more members will take their title a bit too literally and want to *direct* you in solving it. So don't open that door (unless that's what you want).

Let's say you're struggling with hiring. Don't take that information to your board without at least one proposed solution. Two are better. You want their input and the reasoning behind it so you can make an informed decision.

The quickest way to relinquish the mantle of leadership is by planting seeds of doubt within your board about whether you are the best person to wear it. Even if the board likes none of your proposed solutions, you're still illustrating the extent of the problem and your thinking on it—thereby helping to inform theirs.

Which brings us to universal truth number three: *Even when you've established a board and made clear that you are a decisive leader, issues of where the line lies can surface.* In other words, some board members may unilaterally blur (or cross) the line between guidance and operational decision-making.

Even the best-intentioned board members can start reaching in and operationally directing the company. *Unless the leadership team is absolutely broken,* however, that's almost always a bad idea, because it's a short leap from there to utter confusion about who is actually calling the shots.

Corporate boards exist to *provide counsel* on overall strategy— *not* to dictate how strategy is carried out. Their fundamental role is to make sure the company has a sound strategy and to ensure the CEO leading the company is the right person for the job. The CEO's job, meanwhile, is to install the right executive team and staff to carry it out.

VENTURE CAPITAL, PRIVATE EQUITY, AND PUBLIC COMPANY BOARDS

For boards of VC start-ups, I think the primary focus is on finding a good product and good market to go after—put simply, getting the company off the ground. Once that happens, the question becomes, "Can we produce revenue from that market and start creating relatively predictable growth?"

That's not to suggest VC boards don't care about costs—they do. But they're not laser focused on highly detailed cost management. A right-thinking VC board, in my view, tends to be more interested in, "What do we have to invest to get to the growth we think this thing can have?"

As SailPoint scaled in the VC model, we moved from it to PE, which is unusual. Our PE board was much more focused on a disciplined balance of growth and profitability. It was indispensable in helping us move from a growth company to a focus on execution, cost management, and delivering predictable profitability.

We'd sometimes joke about that distinction within the management team: the VC folks were saying, "Grow, grow, *grow*! *And* a little *profit* would be nice!" while the PE board was all, "Profit, profit, *profit*! But we'll also need some *growth*!"

In fact, both were essential. We'd never have gotten off the ground without our strong VC board, and our PE team helped us blend growth with profit in a very healthy way. That ultimately got us to *profitable, sustainable* growth—pretty much the definition of a *real business*.

I wouldn't say going public was SailPoint's objective from the outset, but once we decided to take that step, we experienced a whole new relationship with *yet another* type of board. Our move to public ownership was less dramatic than some, and I credit that largely to our exposure to the PE board; just knowing what was expected and having the discipline to understand the financial picture proved a big help.

But this new board also harkens back to the VC board in a notable way: its balance.

Our VC (start-up) board was composed of three independent venture firms; none owned a majority of the company, but their *combined* positions made up a majority. When we became a majority-owned PE firm, the board essentially spoke with one voice and could pretty much determine what it wanted to happen.

But (outside the "closely held" exceptions) public companies aren't typically owned by anybody. They're *widely* held, and as we executed our IPO and our PE firm reduced its ownership, the board shifted again. It became strongly reminiscent of the more balanced VC board. It was back to multiple voices.

The difference, of course, is that board members of a publicly held company are not investors in a start-up. They're independent; they have a fiduciary responsibility to the *company*, not to themselves. And so the concerns shift still again: diversity becomes a big thing. You want a board that represents a lot of diverse views of the world, and frankly, in VC and PE land, there's less concern with that, although I think that is finally, if sluggishly, changing.

Venture backed or not, no young company wants somebody coming in and stealing its idea.

BEYOND THE BASICS

These universal truths and model-specific traits notwithstanding, there are areas of crossover between the various *types* of boards. A great example is proprietary information. The protection of inside info is crucial within each model but for subtly different reasons.

Venture backed or not, no young company wants somebody coming in and stealing its idea.

At the other end of the continuum, pretty much everybody knows what publicly held firms are working on—but you still want the details about your progress, setbacks, features—to remain nebulous, since all news affects share price (i.e., "investor confidence").

So different reasons, but in both cases (and at every stage of a company's development), the relative importance of protecting information is comparable.

Another example of various business models' shared interrelatedness is the increasing practice of taking public companies private. Dell comes first to mind, of course.

Shifting models as Dell did allows you to restructure and temporarily lose money out of public view. You can leverage investors' maturity and sophistication into an understanding that you're thinking long range and that it starts with getting your house back in order. PE firms do this a lot—but try it on Wall Street, and brows will furrow. Eyes (and quite possibly heads) will roll because of the hyperfocus on quarterly results. It's simply a reality of today's public markets.

So always bear in mind the field you're playing on, and realize that over the life of your company, it is likely to change—perhaps more than once or twice. Using your board properly, whatever the field of play, is a crucial element in determining the best model for what you're doing and for your stage of growth.

BRING YOUR OWN CHAIR

I WRITE ABOUT THE Herman Miller Aeron chair, and all it represented during the dot-com bubble, in "Lead by Example." But there's another piece to the story.

When we were getting things started at SailPoint, not only were the offices not grand (that's putting it mildly), not only did the cofounders share an office (just like everybody else), not only were the desks basic and the walls generally devoid of art—but when we looked at what was happening with the Aeron chair, we purposely went in the opposite direction. The policy was called "BYO chair."

We gave new hires a $200 chair allowance. If someone really wanted to, they could spend $400. But the other $200 was on them.

Our rationale was simple: We're going to give you a good computer, the technology you need. Not a fancy desk or a fancy office. But since you sit most of the day, we'll make sure you have a comfortable chair. Not an Aeron chair—but a *comfortable* chair.

A fun side story: When we hired the first guy who was younger than the rest of us—I think Peter was twenty-nine when he joined us, but he was our "baby"—he did the BYOC thing and spent most of the morning assembling it, just like everybody else had, on his first day. One day when he was out, some of his colleagues headed to Babies "R" Us (or someplace like it) on their lunch hour. They knew what they were looking for, and they wanted it to be *just right*.

I still remember the look on Peter's face the next morning when his BYOC had been "upgraded" by his team.

I wonder if he still has that high chair.

CANDY, NOT KALE

WE'VE HAD CANDY AT SailPoint since day one. It was essential in our start-up phase, and it stuck. But every so often, now that we're established, we'll get somebody who's like, "Hey, you know what? We need healthier stuff."

So once, as an experiment—*only* once, it turns out—we took the candy bowls away.

The result was pretty much open revolt. You would have thought we cut salaries 50 percent across the board. The internal emails said, "Put the candy bowls back! This is terrible! We can't code without candy."

So naturally—being the loving, caring management team we are—we brought the candy back.

Now we joke with new people, "Watch out for the Freshman 15! That free candy will kick your butt if you let it!"

But I'll say this: when we brought candy back, it came back with a *vengeance*. Candy in every conference room. Candy in the lobby. Families of new employees would come in for a tour, and it was like Willy Wonka had thrown open the factory doors: "You've got *free candy* in *every room?*"

So we're back where we started: candy bowls in the break room only. Although now it's not in bowls but in a number of drawers. (Our employee population is larger, and the break room's a much bigger place these days.)

But at least people have to make the trek to get their fix. And very, very rarely does someone ask us to swap out the candy for kale.

CELEBRITY OR CEO?

WHEN I ASKED BILL, the chair of SailPoint's board of directors, about doing this project, I got exactly the response I'd hoped for: "As long as it does absolutely nothing to derail your focus on the business, sure."

A lot of people write books to burnish—or build—reputations, often with one eye on post-C-suite careers, whether as consultants, motivational speakers, authors, or all of these. I wrote this one because I have a genuine interest in helping start-ups and young organizations get the order of things right.

It's a passion I've tried to capture throughout this book. (*See* "Values, *Then* Vision" and "Idea? Feature? Product? Business?")

Getting priorities right is such a big factor in every venture's success that it's impossible to overstate. I've mentored enough leaders of young companies (and would-be companies) here in Austin to know this much at least: the correlation between having your priorities right and the chances of success isn't merely striking. It is absolute.

When I told Bill I was thinking of writing this book, he was doing for me what I try to do for those young entrepreneurs: making sure *I* kept true to what matters. His response was better proof than

The correlation between having your priorities right and the chances of success isn't merely striking. It is absolute.

I can put in writing of how doing things in the right order creates and furthers a company's culture. Still, many companies try to create culture first and hope it produces the right values.

It just doesn't work that way.

CONTENT VERSUS CONTEXT

WHEN I'M TALKING TO younger people about their career paths—although I think this is helpful for people at any stage of their vocational lives—I tell them it boils down to two ideas: *content*, or what you're working on, and *context*, or where you're doing it. It's oversimplified, but with that caveat in place, sales provides a perfect example of this distinction in action.

Salesman A sells used cars. Saleswoman—umm, okay, I guess we don't need the letters after all—sells large enterprise computer networks. Both are in sales, but their jobs' contexts have almost nothing in common.

The car guy is totally transactional. You walk in with your daughter, who needs a reliable ride for college. That's what this interaction means *to you*. But from the salesman's point of view, it's about one thing: *closing*. Making the sale within forty-five minutes of the introductory handshake. If that doesn't happen, he's probably lost you. He's unlikely ever to talk to you again, and you'll probably never talk to him again. End of relationship.

The sale's value doesn't even approach that of an enterprise computer network. But neither is a car a trivial purchase. It's a pretty big dollar amount. Yet we do it in this very fast, fairly transactional way.

Our computer sales professional takes a whole different approach. She *actually is* building a relationship. She must, because whether she makes the sale or not, she'll be talking to the organization *for the rest of her life.* If she gets the order, it'll be as her company's ambassador to the client firm; if not, she'll keep plugging away at them. Again, a night-and-day *contextual* difference to our car salesman.

A lot of people think they are natural salespersons. "I'm great; I can sell anything to anybody." But all they've homed in on is what the *content* of their working life will be. Context is just as important, arguably more so.

When I'm talking to young folks about tech, they tend to visualize their work involving science or math more than English. But it's *not enough* to know that you like working on math or science (or for that matter, English)—using Microsoft-speak, this means determining whether you're an Excel, PowerPoint, or Word person. That's only half of what you need to be thinking about.

All of this has much more to do with management and leadership and culture than it may at first seem. Getting *those* things right depends deeply on the extent to which your people are doing the things *they* like (and therefore do) best—*and* that they are doing them in the right arenas, the right places. The right contexts.

If you're fresh out of college, should you work in a start-up or a big established company? A structured environment or a less-structured one?

Just because you have your degree doesn't mean you should jump at the best offer you get. On the contrary—and again, it's true *throughout* our vocational lives—you need to choose your employer as carefully as you did your field of study and *where* you studied it. Did you go to a liberal arts school with four hundred students or a giant university with sixty thousand? Yes, both are universities, but that's where their similarities end. They're going to provide two *very* different experiences.

As leaders, one of the most important things we can do to assure our companies' success is to place a priority on getting our people as close as possible to their ideal work contents *and* contexts. Because whatever our career stage, we all do our best when we're doing *what* we love in the *right* place.

> *You need to choose your employer as carefully as you did your field of study and* where *you studied it.*

DELEGATION

AS LEADERS, WE FALL short when we don't do the mission-critical things only we can do because we're still spending time on things we *like* to do, things we *used* to do, or things we *can* do instead. We tend to do these sorts of things when we have one or more of the following: the *time*, the *inclination*, or a *lack of trust.*

If you lead an organization and seriously believe you have sufficient *time* to do anything other than the things that your position alone requires you to do, let me disabuse you of that belief once and for all: you don't.

If you have the *inclination* to do something you used to do, it isn't important whether that inclination is born of dissatisfaction with how that thing is now being done. All that matters is whether you have the fortitude to *resist doing it*, because your role as a leader demands you to.

And if you *lack trust* that someone you've hired to take direction from you and produce a given result can or will do so, as much as I hate to say it, you're probably not a leader—because leadership is about trusting the process. It's not about *holding on* to control; it's about *letting it go*: letting go of doing things yourself and developing the trust that other people will figure it out. (*See* "You, the Conductor.")

I'm not suggesting these demands of you as a leader are not difficult. They are, and because they are, leaders both experienced and new sometimes escape to their comfort zones and justify doing so with a simple, "Well, I like to do this."

Maybe we think about that next business trip and the seat we want on the plane—and the next thing we know, we've spent fifteen minutes we'll never get back, booking the travel ourselves. Because *getting that window seat* was a lot more fun than lighting fires under the butts of those who have put off tackling that problem over in accounting (or marketing or engineering or sales or ...) for so long.

Leading can often be fun, but sometimes it isn't. The best leaders understand and accept this and consistently resist the temptation to do anything *other* than lead by (1) recognizing the importance of their time and what they spend it on; (2) resisting the urge to do something because they can; and (3) developing trust in their subordinates by giving them the space to make mistakes—and ultimately, to figure things out. (*See* "Priorities, Setting.")

DISRUPTION—AND DYSFUNCTION

IF YOU WANT TO be an innovator, I think you have a decision to make: whether you want to be an *inventive* innovator or a *disruptive* innovator.

Despite its ubiquity today, the word *disruption*, used in reference to products, ideas, and processes that produce fundamental change, has been around a lot longer than most people (those outside of tech, at least) realize. Further, that word by itself accounts for only half of what has been called the most influential business idea of this century.

The idea's full name is *disruptive innovation*. It was first described by Clayton Christensen in 1995 and fully explained in his groundbreaking 1997 book, *The Innovator's Dilemma*.

The use of *disruption* to describe everything (it seems), from new ice cream flavors to *truly* disruptive innovations, didn't really show up in the wider world for another decade.

Then, in 2017, a team of Malaysian researchers defined a disruptive innovation as one that "creates a new value network and eventually disrupts an existing one, displacing established market-leading firms, products, and alliances."[1]

That's a pretty tall order, and it's fraught with wider social and ethical implications.

What's often overlooked is that innovation takes many forms. Just because you don't break and remake markets doesn't mean you're not an innovator. And let's not forget that putting pressure on yourself and your people to create earth-shatteringly disruptive innovations pretty much guarantees failure.

Both of which sum up my interpretation of Christensen's book: there are healthy and unhealthy ways to (try to) create change.

Thanks to the pace of technological change—what's now called the *digital transformation of business*—all businesses everywhere are getting transformed but not always for the better. It's one reason Amazon (and Google and Facebook) is scary to almost everyone on the planet. They're using digital technology to change practically every industry, and in so doing, they often force those industries to conform to the changes they impose—although a strong argument can be made that nobody knows what changes a given industry needs better than the people working in it.

Fortunately, as I write, Silicon Valley has embarked on a journey of introspection on a scale not previously seen. People *outside* of tech have been asking for years if the industry has gone too far, but at last, many *within* it are asking the same questions: What is the morality and what are the ethics of creating apps that keep people staring at their phones and other screens? What can we do to reverse salary structures that have put housing in San Francisco beyond the

---

1   Ab Rahman, Airini; et al., "Emerging Technologies with Disruptive Effects: A Review," PERINTIS eJournal 7 (2), retrieved December 21, 2017.

reach of almost everyone not working in tech? Are the devices we've created, ostensibly to connect us, coming at the price of actual, direct human connection? And while tremendous convenience comes from various organizations knowing enough about us to suggest a product or content that may appeal to us before we even ask for it, should we just ignore the threat this poses in terms of maintaining our privacy?

These questions revolve not around whether disruption *itself* is a good thing; it almost always *can* be. They're about *where the line* lies between disruption and dysfunction. And increasing numbers of people are pointing to places where they feel that line has been crossed.

If that's true, the question morphs again: What *degree* of disruption do we want to pursue? Do we really want to leave massive ugliness in our wake? Ugliness takes many forms, from treating workers really badly within the innovation *process* itself to the societal effects of the *innovations* we unleash.

Simply in trying to be an innovator, it's a given that you're trying to create disruption at some level. But take it too far, and it becomes a short leap from innovation to inanity, disruption to dysfunction.

Simply in trying to be an innovator, it's a given that you're trying to create disruption at some level. But take it too far, and it becomes a short leap from innovation to inanity, disruption to dysfunction.

So which will it be: *inventive* innovator or *disruptive* innovator?

There is no one right answer, but the ethical and moral implications of the latter are only increasing—so you'd best factor them in before you choose.

DONNA, PRIMA

I HAVE WORKED WITH some incredibly talented people. None is more trying than those who constantly let you know about it, whom we sometimes call *prima donnas*.

There are savants in every field, and watching them at work can be breathtaking. But not when *they're* the ones sucking the air out of the room. That quickly becomes debilitating for *everyone else* in the room.

So by all means, bring in talented people. Lots of them. Just avoid the cocky, prima donna types. They're never, ever worth it.

EXCEPTIONS

IN "FOUR I'S, THE" I dissect the set of values upon which SailPoint was built. But as sure as the sun rises and sets each day, someone reading this book is bound to say, "Mark, please. I've worked with someone from SailPoint who was a real jerk."

Hey, there are exceptions to every rule, and our instant-rating world illustrates this in real time, every day. No matter how strong your values are, you'll mess up at times.

We are very proud of having scaled as quickly as we did without it affecting our rating on Glassdoor, for example. But sure enough, even there, we've received some negative comments. I'm good with that, because nobody's perfect. That's true no matter what you're talking about. As we all know, it's the very existence of exceptions that often proves a broader rule.

But it goes further.

Exceptions can convince us to look at things from a different angle. Statistical data, for instance, are important in understanding what's going on but also in showing very early when something's changed—and not necessarily for the worse. Exceptions can and often do point to *new* areas of research and toward the development of new solutions.

So don't write them off. Exceptions are challenges we have not yet addressed. Without them, exactly what would we do all day long?

FAMILY, ONE BIG HAPPY

A LOT OF ORGANIZATIONS make a big deal about how their people are connected across departments and skill sets, about the transcendence of a "family atmosphere" that exists within their walls.

I get this—or at least the desire to convey it.

But I also think there's danger in stating it, because there often seems to exist an inverse relationship between the true sense of connectedness people within big organizations feel and management's claims of connectedness among workers. This probably has to do with the fact that the more we try to force things on employees, the harder some will resist.

Let's be honest: coworkers are not family, any more than actual family members you meet for the first time at a giant family reunion and never see again are family. (I've never been to a family reunion of that scale myself, but they're out there. We've all seen the T-shirts: "75th Smith Family Reunion. We may barely know each other, but it's a great excuse for a party!")

Yes, all these Smiths share a common bloodline, but that's about it.

We all have something in common, but the bigger a company gets, the less it's going to feel like a family in the immediate sense of that word.

Work is the same: we all have something in common, but the bigger a company gets, the less it's going to feel like a family in the immediate sense of that word. Compounding this truth is another, that growth itself is antithetical to feeling small and connected.

Smart companies therefore leverage broader, shared values as common ground on which workers can connect to whatever degree they are comfortable. I've found one of the best places for doing that is through service to the community *beyond* our company's walls.

You may never get that engineer and salesperson to agree that demand is reliant upon customer pain. (Engineers typically believe that if something works great and is sufficiently cool, sales will follow. Salespeople, meanwhile, counter that if it isn't addressing something widely seen as problematic in the first place, it doesn't matter how well it works or cool it is; there's no incentive to buy.)

Similarly, you won't get people in other parts of your company to agree on some other work-specific things. But if your culture encourages people to stand shoulder to shoulder and work for some greater good—ladling out meals at a soup kitchen, helping with a blood drive, building a house with Habitat for Humanity, whatever it may be—they'll at least get the chance to forget their differing work perspectives and perhaps understand and appreciate each other as fellow humans, doing good for other fellow humans.

That can only be a good thing, and the difference you'll see in intracompany harmony is the icing on the cake.

FIGHT FAIR

PEOPLE IN THE BUSINESS world change teams regularly. Companies get bought and sold. People move from company to company. They might move to a vendor or to one of your customers.

So don't to be a jerk. Fight fair.

Business is like pickup basketball. We're on the same team this game, and in the next game, we're opponents. If you were a jerk in the last game, I don't really want you on my team.

A lot of the people we recruit from other companies say the same thing: "At my last job, we all respected the caliber of your products, but you have this great reputation as a good place to work and for treating people right."

> *Business is like pickup basketball. We're on the same team this game, and in the next game, we're opponents.*

Competing means fighting hard but fighting fair. If you fight cheap or dirty, word will get around, and the people you want to come work for you won't do it.

FOUR I'S, THE

MAYBE THE MOST EXCITING facet of deciding to embark on your own venture is the opportunity it offers to take what you've seen and learned before that moment and create something new that applies those lessons in a whole new way. Specifically, *yours*.

I know my cofounders at my first start-up, Waveset Technologies, would agree. We didn't necessarily see it at the time, but the culture we created was heavily influenced by our reactions to—okay, I'll say it, *against*—some of the things we saw happening at other organizations.

Topping the list for me is how larger established organizations seem over time to be where innovation goes to die.

When a company has enjoyed great success for many years and has products all over the marketplace, there is a tendency to say, "Well, we've got this licked." In such companies' defense, it happens so gradually—almost organically—that it seemingly comes out of nowhere. But pretty soon you're not listening to the customer as well. Though your products are out in the marketplace, your people are not, not as much as necessary at least, listening to customer pain, which is the fuel of creativity and promotes aggressiveness in

Innovation means understanding customer challenges and pain points and developing creative solutions to them.

dreaming up new solutions to it.

My Waveset founders and I identified four areas where this manifests, and we decided to make them main areas of our focus—barometers for how we were doing, not just in the early stages but as we grew and eventually became a mature organization. They've carried through at SailPoint, and it's with zero hyperbole that I assure you of this: *more than anything else we've done, these four values have been responsible for the success of both organizations.*

We called them the Four I's: innovation, integrity, impact, and individuals. And we distilled the importance of each in just a few words.

INNOVATION: WE DEVELOP CREATIVE SOLUTIONS TO REAL CUSTOMER CHALLENGES.

Over time, many companies get into kind of a dull, repetitive pattern, where their innovations tend to be far less effective. Others do a great job of staying innovative, and we figured out pretty early that identifying innovation as a primary mission would allow us to constantly reinforce it, to reinvent our best solutions when they require it, and to keep us on the lookout for new opportunities to innovate.

Innovation means understanding customer challenges and pain points and developing creative solutions to them. It's an amalgam of product marketing and product management skills, of listening to the market, and of engineering people who can take a problem and figure out how to solve it. We essentially said, "Project management plus engineering equals innovation."

And then we looked at it organizationally in terms of value. Although we articulated it within product development aimed at customers initially, we said, "Look, innovation applies *everywhere*.

We should be innovative about how we contract, how we sell, how we market."

We never wanted our legal team to get too innovative, of course, because you know, that might involve jail ... for me—no fun.

But we wanted everybody in the company, even those serving internal customers—finance and accounting and purchasing—to still be innovative in how they solved their problems. Give them an easier way to turn in receipts, to specify equipment needed. The core value is innovation.

For new organizations starting out, the proof in the pudding of innovation, especially in the business-to-business (B2B) world, is that whatever solution you're offering has to be innovative in a fundamental, pretty much disruptive way (*see* "Disruption—and Dysfunction"), because if your solution looks, feels, and sounds kind of like something customers can get or already are getting from a big established company, that's what they'll do every time. They're not going to risk going with an unproven young company if your solution looks and/or performs like what they're already getting, but if it feels unique and different, they'll at least take a look, which pretty much defines the value of innovation: it's what gets your foot in the door, and then you have to deliver real value. (*See* "Products, Good and Not So Good.")

INTEGRITY: WE DELIVER ON THE COMMITMENTS WE MAKE.

Something else we noticed about big companies was their tendency to overpromise and underdeliver, to not follow through on what they say they're going to do. That's a failure to deliver, pure and simple, even when (and if) delivery eventually occurs. Worse, it takes value completely out of the equation.

A lot of people see integrity as synonymous with honesty and consider honesty just table stakes—the price of admission. Without honesty and the *trust* it fosters, there is no relationship; I don't care if we're talking business, personal, or otherwise.

But we take integrity further. We see it as consistently making and following through on our commitments. It's a higher bar, and here's why.

If I promise you something and don't deliver, I've destroyed trust. If I consistently underpromise and overdeliver, however, you're really going to like working with me, because I've earned your trust not through my words but *through my actions*. In fact, this type of behavior leads to the elusive concept of "delighting" our customers. We all love to be surprised in a positive way, and nothing is more positive than exceeding our expectations.

The critical corollary that big companies too often either forget or no longer care about is the value of *accumulated trust* when things go awry. Because it happens. Even with the best intent in the world, there are times you aren't able to deliver what you were confident you could. Whether the context is a personal or business relationship, the priority at that moment is *communication*. The minute you know you'll be unable to deliver is when you tell people—and I don't mean via a text or email. At minimum pick up the phone, and if they're close by, go see them.

People hate nothing more than last-minute *negative* surprises, and no last-minute surprise is more hated than a failed delivery. If you know in advance, which (if you're paying attention) you almost always do, and you tell people *the moment* you know it, the vast majority will be reasonable and rational.

There will be those who are not. Often there will be warning signs—ridiculous penalties for failure to deliver written into contracts spring to mind—but whatever they are, and whenever you see them, ask yourself if the potential angst is worth the trouble. Almost without exception, it is not.

Most people are reasonable and rational *if* you go to them as early as possible and say, "Hey, I thought I was going to be able to do this by here. It looks like I won't be able to follow through on that. What can we do to create the best possible outcome now?"

The key phrase? *As early as possible.* I can tell you from personal experience that the sooner they know, the better the outcome will be, because schedule juggling on their end to accommodate the delay on yours is often an option.

But the longer you wait, the less likely it becomes.

And so it—integrity—comes down to a very simple rule: *bad news can't wait.*

Has someone, a contractor let's say, ever called you the day that they were due to begin a project and said, "I'm sorry, but there's no way I can get there for another month"? If so, how did you react? You know (short of a sudden illness) that they didn't just figure this out. After calming down, you'd probably have one question, and one only: "Why didn't you tell me sooner, so I could *make other plans?*"

Had the contractor simply done that, he may well have gotten to you sooner than his worst-case scenario. You'd still have been disappointed initially but marginally happier when he showed up sooner than expected.

Instead, that ship has sailed with you aboard, bidding your *former* contractor *adieu.*

IMPACT: WE MEASURE AND REWARD RESULTS, NOT ACTIVITY.

Large legacy companies are often loaded with people who are just taking up space and collecting a paycheck. It's a significant issue, and it goes hand in hand with integrity. We're still talking about overpromising and underdelivering but internally.

Earlier I talked about the necessity of making innovation a priority with internal as well as external customers. The same goes for impact. (For that matter, integrity too.) Effective workers know the difference between busywork and producing value. They find nothing more frustrating than coworkers who stir up a cloud of dust and confuse it with progress.

Everybody in the organization must be clear on what success looks like, and self-starting employees are often clear on that, right out of the gate. Indeed, keeping them *in* the gate is the challenge. So the role of management is to be clear on the objectives and then let people run.

Yet corporate culture—specifically, the received wisdom of the traditional HR industry—says that people's performances must be regularly evaluated with heavy-handed "corporate" forms. The reality is that managers should be more focused on *coaching*, not evaluating, true self-starting, high-value employees. Once given high-level direction, the self-starters we all want on our teams tend to know intuitively what's expected of them and how they're tracking against that standard, provided everyone is clear and open and transparent with them at all times.

If the manager and the employee know what the results are intended to be, it becomes obvious pretty quickly that the employee is either getting those results or is not.

Something else we've learned with impact is that there are times when you must absolutely acknowledge that you've given people "stretch" goals and that not getting the desired result in those cases may be quite acceptable, since you're stretching them toward something more. The trick is to be clear *which type* of goal you're setting up: concrete or aspirational. It feels to me that, when we're firing on all cylinders, we'll get close to our aspirational goals, and we'll hit and exceed the concrete ones. The times when goals that should have been hit and were not then become rare exceptions.

At SailPoint, we know something has gone very wrong for our people when they miss achievable targets. They are that good, and they are that good because they know what was expected from day one (*see* "Put Your Mouth Where Their Money Is").

INDIVIDUALS: WE VALUE EVERY PERSON.

This is the one thing that has changed the most in my thirty-five years in the business world. More and more, companies get that every employee is a whole person. That if we want the best out of them for our companies, we must treat them as the whole people they are—because thanks to technology, the line between home and work has become very fuzzy.

You have this device. You're checking it all the time. You're taking work email at home and personal calls at work. I remember a time when company resources were expressly forbidden for personal use, like making a personal phone call from my desk phone. Or when we first got computers, sending my family an email from my work account was not really okay.

That's all out the window.

As companies, we now pay professionals to get their work done.

We're increasingly less concerned with how—provided, of course, that it's legal and ethical. There are no time clocks. There are few limits. There are no managers watching over a brood of employees as if they were kindergarteners.

We treat people like adults; indeed, at SailPoint, we can shorthand our entire culture to just that: "Treat people like adults." Tell them what you want them to do, give them freedom and resources to do it, then mostly stay out of their way and let them get the job done.

In fact, I often refer to the two guardrails I think managers should bring to leading their people. First, never, ever micromanage a competent professional. While it may make sense to take that approach with a high-school fast-food worker, well-educated, experienced people generally won't put up with it for long and will "vote with their feet" to find somewhere else to work where they won't be treated like a kid. On the other end of the spectrum, a manager needs to define what success looks like at some level, so that their team members are at least pointed in the right direction for what's expected. Then they are free to use their intelligence, experience, and creativity to get their work done. And generally, that's what creates the elusive engagement that employees so desperately crave at work.

When you combine that with respect and valuing their whole person, they will go through walls for you—because they know you will for them. (If you haven't yet, take a moment right now to read "Valuing People versus Claiming To.")

Treating people like *whole* people means not saying, "Oh, you've got this thing going on in your personal life? *Tough crap.* That deadline is a *deadline*. You've got to deliver."

There are still companies out there doing that, but I don't expect they'll be getting away with it much longer. One of the reasons you work around people's personal lives is the knowledge that one day, maybe six months or six years from now, you'll have to look them in the eye and say, "I need you to work a couple of weekends here, because we're really crunched. Can you do that?"

* * *

I can say with *absolute confidence* that instituting the Four I's will not prevent your new company from making mistakes—and plenty of them. They will, however, keep everyone pulling in the same direction and ultimately create a culture that you, your customers, and your employees, investors, vendors, and board will appreciate and aspire to uphold and deepen.

FRUGALITY FAIL

AT ONE OF MY start-ups (I've withheld the name to protect the guilty), one of my cofounders decided to save some time and money by holding out on buying a filing cabinet.

We had only a few things on paper anyway—we're in tech, after all. What we did have had been sent to us. By the state.

One night the custodian came through, and when we came in the next morning, all the color drained from my cofounder's face.

The documents—our articles of incorporation—were gone.

We all learned a tough lesson: protect the important stuff.

I'm pretty sure none of us will ever temporarily store important documents in a *blue wastebasket* ever again.

FUN WITH NUMBERS

LIKE A LOT OF leaders, I've leaned on other leaders and thinkers to fuel my own approaches to both life and business challenges with some simple rules of thumb. Here are a few based on numbers that I especially like, lightning-round style.

THE 80-20 RULE

You probably know (or have at least heard of) this one.

Also called the Pareto Principle, this popular axiom is generally interpreted to mean that 80 percent of outcomes result from 20 percent of actions. It was named for a man widely considered a seminal influence on modern economic theory, but when Vilfredo Pareto first published his foundational finding in the late nineteenth century—that 80 percent of Italy's land was owned by 20 percent of its population—its ubiquity wasn't yet clear, leaving his fame far from assured.

> *The 80-20 Rule: 80 percent of outcomes result from 20 percent of actions.*

Only as later generations discovered the 80-20 rule's influence on areas far beyond property ownership was Pareto lauded as its progenitor.

Today, it's an acknowledgment that a large proportion of the impacts in many arenas comes from a much smaller degree of input or from a relatively small number of participants working for change. And intuitively, most of us know that to be true—which, I suppose, explains why we cite Pareto all the time.

95-5—DOING VERSUS REFLECTING

A few years ago I was counseled to make sure I spent about 5 percent of my time in reflection.

Many of us just run, run, run. Every so often, you need to step away, to take a hiatus from the day to day, and to ask: *Am I working on the right stuff? Do I have the right people on the bus? Are they in the right seats?* There are lots of metaphors and plenty of business-world catchphrases that allude to this, but something about how it was presented to me just captured it.

Leader or not, each of us can and absolutely should spend about 95 percent of our time executing. But if we don't carve out 5 percent for thought and reflection, we risk getting on and hurtling down the wrong track without even realizing it. Or as John Dewey put it, "We do not learn from experience … we learn from reflecting on experience."

80-10-10—LIVING WITH MARGIN AND GIVING TO OTHERS

This one comes primarily from the Bible. It's tied to the rule of tithing, of giving 10 percent of your income to the church or those in need or however you define "the greater good."

Most of us would do well to live on 80 percent of what we make, save 10 percent, and give that last 10 percent to other causes. Unfortunately, a lot of us live on 110 percent, save nothing, give nothing, and keep those profits rolling in for the credit card companies.

This idea of margin and giving applies just the same to our time and energy as it does to our money. If I can give 10 percent of my time to good causes and reserve 10 percent for personal and family "refreshment and renewal," I'm probably living a better, more balanced life.

My own thinking on this extends beyond our personal lives, however, to our companies. In other chapters, I discuss the benefits to organizations of giving back. There are many, not least that a consistent ethic of supporting the communities in which we work benefits them *and* the connections within our organizations.

If every company encouraged its employees to give 10 percent of their time to a cause they care about, imagine the difference it could make in our communities and our society. And in the lives of our *employees* too.

95-5 (V.2)—OWNING YOUR SHARE OF THE BLAME

Coming again from my Christian perspective for a moment, there's a book I read years ago, Ken Sande's *The Peacemaker*, that shared a direct, worthwhile approach to conflict resolution.

Sande said we tend to think we should apologize in a conflict situation only when we're convinced that we own at least 50 percent of the problem. If I'm pretty sure you own 90 and I own 10, or worse, you own 95 and I own maybe 5, it's easy to feel like, "Hey, why should *I* apologize? It's all on *him*." But that's not entirely accurate, is it?

Instead, Sande says, we actually make the situation better almost immediately simply by acknowledging our role in it, however small it may be. And beyond that, my own takeaway was that we get past it even more quickly when we own most of it and just say so. If we can just remove emotion and pride from the equation as early as possible, we get right to the resolution and get on to more important things.

The really beautiful part of this to me is that even if the other person *never* gets to owning their part, at least you've owned yours and can move forward knowing that. Anyone who has been involved in conflict directly or even viewed it at close range knows that there's always the sense that both parties have some responsibility for it. Sande's point is that the sooner you own yours, the more likely the other person will own theirs.

So be the first to acknowledge your share in a conflict. And— this is important—though I've described it here in percentage terms, you *don't* want to break it out that way *in real life*. Telling the other person, "Hey, I think this is 95 percent on you … " Yeah, probably not a good idea.

THE 40-70 RULE—PLANNING VERSUS EXECUTING

Popularized by former secretary of state and retired four-star general Colin Powell, the 40-70 rule is a great hedge against both impulsive decision-making and its opposite, paralysis by analysis.

Powell saw the information-gathering stage of the decision-making process as running along a continuum, beginning with insufficient information and ending with too much. His 40-70 rule holds that once you have at least 40 percent of the critical information and a strong gut instinct about how to go, it's usually okay to follow that instinct.

What if you're still unsure? No problem: Keep gathering information until you develop some certainty. Once you have 70 percent of the crucial info, however, you have to move. Waiting longer, on the off chance that the remaining 30 percent of information will negate what is already the preponderance of facts, amounts to dithering.

And while leaders come in a variety of types, ditherer isn't one of them.

One of Powell's four-star forerunners said essentially the same thing more succinctly:

"A good plan, violently executed now, is better than a perfect plan next week."

—*Gen. George S. Patton*

FUNDING AND PIVOTS

ELSEWHERE I DISCUSS THE importance, before seeking VC, of careful planning and analyzing what you think may be an idea for a new business. Without (and often *with*) a fully fleshed-out plan, it's likely your idea won't sustain a business over the long term (*see* "Idea? Feature? Product? Business?").

Here's another question, one that those proposing a new venture seldom think about but that investors do all the time: "Are we investing in an idea or in a team?"

The answer is sometimes one, sometimes the other. An incredibly brilliant idea can sometimes be enough to secure funding. An investor will say, "I don't know if this guy or this team is going to be able to execute it, but that's a great idea. Let's get it going."

At some point down the road, a seasoned team may be brought in to develop it, if the person or team who came up with it proves unable to. It happens all the time: the initial entrepreneur begins to struggle with the increasing challenges of scale and complexity, and it's time to bring in the leaders with experience at growing and scaling a business.

Conversely, and to be blunt, our teams at both Waveset and

SailPoint probably got funding because we looked bankable. We got a clear sense from our investors that "this set of people—they'll probably figure it out." And the reason that we and others have been able to do that can be summed up with one word: pivot.

It's a popular term now but one that has applied to start-ups since the beginning of commerce itself: the willingness to listen to markets and respond, to be market driven (*see* "Markets, Listening To").

Investors are naturally more trusting of teams that are not only well versed in their fields of endeavor but that strive to define the problems they are trying to solve in very clear, precise terms.

Investors are naturally more trusting of teams that are not only well versed in their fields of endeavor but that strive to define the problems they are trying to solve in very clear, precise terms.

So they define the problem and head down a path toward solving it—but often they realize, as they listen to the market and understand the issue even more deeply, that they had 50 percent of it right but 50 percent wrong.

At this point, lesser teams will do one of two bad things: (1) put their heads down and plow ahead, ignoring the warning signs that they don't have it all right (which often results in a *Thelma and Louise*–type ending to their start-up as they sail off the cliff); or (2) throw up their hands in confusion and chaos, when what's needed is an even stronger commitment. Solving the issues that you identify in that previously unknown 50 percent is what's likely to get you over the top.

It may mean changing to a different market or slightly refining features, but if you do what it takes to get it absolutely right, you'll be well on the way to success—for your team and for the people who funded you.

GIVING BACK

VERY EARLY, BOTH SAILPOINT and Waveset committed preliquidity equity to the Entrepreneurs Foundation of Central Texas.

This organization and others like it around the country encourage early-stage companies to donate stock that will hopefully someday become a way to help society. If there's a liquidity event— the company is sold, goes IPO, whatever it may be—the stock turns into real money, usually set up as a donor-directed fund.

When will it happen? Who knows?

But we made the commitment—and in the meantime, we encouraged our people to give back to the community in the form of sweat equity. Work teams headed out regularly, perhaps one Friday every month or two, to do good works, creating a benefit not just for the recipient of their efforts but back at the office too.

Working for a common good is a great way to unite employees of disparate disciplines. It promotes even stronger cooperation in work matters, which, in turn, hastens company growth, making that preliquidity equity we've pledged that much closer to becoming liquid one day.

This is just one approach corporations can take in engaging in

Working for a common good is a great way to unite employees of disparate disciplines.

philanthropy, the expectation of which is only—and in my opinion, rightly—increasing within the general public. It's no longer enough to say your company cares. You have to walk the talk.

Marc Benioff of Salesforce has done much in this regard. Salesforce's 1-1-1 model of corporate philanthropy encourages companies to pledge 1 percent each of their products, time, and resources to worthy causes. "The business of business is improving the state of the world," Benioff says, and I agree wholeheartedly.

Both Waveset and SailPoint went with the Entrepreneurs Foundation because of the way it leverages our everyday efforts into a potential windfall down the road. Both times, it paid off for Central Texas: first when Waveset was sold and more recently with SailPoint's IPO. Both created a nice chunk of funds that the companies could determine how to give away. Real cash that was given to organizations working to help people in need.

I believe giving back must be a value from day one, not a promise to be made good on only when (and if) your company makes it.

By ingraining that value in your company's culture as early as possible, you *ensure* a positive impact—even though start-ups, running on their founders' mortgage-backed loans and maxed-out credit cards and other people's investments, are obviously not positioned to give away money.

What they can offer is something every charity needs and most find hard to get: people on the ground, pitching in, doing actual work. This benefits both the charity and the organization, which shows right from the start that its commitment to the community is not just talk.

Couple this sweat equity with the promise of *real* equity when your liquidity event occurs, and your company is helping at the two most crucial times: now *and* later.

HEADHUNTERS

AS A COMPANY GROWS beyond its founders' and employees' network of potential hires, and particularly when it comes to critical, senior-level hires, executive search firms (a.k.a. headhunters) can be indispensable. *Provided* you never lose ownership of the process.

Outsourcing is a fraught term in business these days, with good reason. Headhunting is an example whose core lessons, I believe, are transferrable across the outsourcing spectrum.

That's because people—meaning customers (both internal and external), vendors, and PE and VC firms; basically anyone or any organization your company has contact with—*don't care* if you hire out help. In fact, if you do it right, they won't even *know* you have.

But do it wrong, and they'll know instantly—because the service they get runs so afoul of the values and culture you've worked so hard to establish and uphold. When that happens, it's *not* on the company you've outsourced to. *It's on you.*

With headhunters in particular, the sales pitch is often that they match candidates to both the competencies you require *and* your corporate culture. Sounds great, right? But does it actually happen?

The answer *can* be yes—provided your core cultural or talent

Think of hired services as augmenting what you've always done, not taking it over.

team is heavily involved. That's really the only way to ensure that the candidates you short-list are truly tied into your values.

I'm talking here about something that supersedes competence and even culture. I'm talking about *chemistry*.

If you outsource something and the firm you engage isn't fully committed to fulfilling the requirements that you have established, it will not go well. There is one and only one way to ensure the contracted service maintains that level of commitment: by *keeping your people involved* throughout the process. And it's every bit as true with search firms as it is for anything else you contract out.

Think of hired services as *augmenting* what you've always done, *not* taking it over. Because unless they fully live and breathe your culture—which, by definition, no outsourced service does—they will never do it with the same focus on culture as you.

HEALTHY (AND UNHEALTHY) TENSION

WE ALL LIVE WITH tension, but not all tension is bad.

In the chapter "Tensions (versus Problems)," I discuss realities that come with doing business and inherent tensions we must manage and how to discern them from problems we must solve. Here, I'm concerned with our more familiar concept of tension: the pressures we put on ourselves and the stressors that often surface between individuals and teams.

Again, such tension is not always in itself a bad thing. Many of us can (and do) get so stressed about doing things well, or completely, or perfectly, or before the deadline, or whatever it is that we're unable to function. Clearly, that's unhealthy tension. But if you let yourself get lackadaisical and complacent, that's unhealthy too.

Individually, we all need a *healthy* amount of tension in our lives, or maybe determined, goal-oriented action is a better concept. This idea applies to anything demanding: physical training, mental toughness, emotional resiliency, and spiritual development.

Similarly, there is healthy and unhealthy tension at work. It can arise between individuals, between teams, or within teams. But arise it will, and that much you can be sure of. So when do you let people disagree, maybe even get into arguments?

Provided they're arguing over concepts and best approaches to the challenges of their work objectives, the answer is *all the time.* Only good can come from open, and even emphatic, discussion of the best way to accomplish things. But ...

That's not always human nature, is it? There's often an unhealthy tension between coworkers and within or between teams, where people go passive-aggressive. Rather than hash it out in direct dialogue, they go off behind people's backs and crucify them. Or when they do talk it out, they resort to screaming and yelling and even name-calling.

The presence—or lack—of this kind of tension speaks to leadership. To organizational culture, the type of tension you allow to manifest says a lot about your company. If you allow people to scream and yell and throw things at each other—whether names or actual objects—good people won't want to stay in that environment, because it's just not healthy.

If you drive the *healthy* tension underground, however, you can get that passive-aggressiveness, when people are nice to each other in public but terrible behind each other's backs—those dysfunctional, office-politics-fraught environments that ultimately implode.

Now don't get me wrong. This isn't necessarily an either-or proposition. Some organizations with lots of tension and competition in their cultures do well, and others where things are more collegial and collaborative do well. But Andy Grove, who played a big role in making Intel great, got it as close to right as I have seen with an approach that became known as "Disagree and Commit."

His thing essentially was that we would vehemently argue, we would get every idea out there, and we would make sure we turned over every option. He encouraged people to play devil's advocate, to try to shoot holes in every approach before it was adopted. But then when we hashed it all out and exited as a team, we would *all commit* to what we decided.

If you were on the wrong side of the ultimate decision, *you still committed.* You wouldn't go passive-aggressive, nod and smile in the meeting, and then go off to your group and start undermining the course that had been agreed to because it wasn't your idea, right?

I think Grove's point was that most companies get it backward: they seek agreement in the meeting but let people decommit outside the meeting, when the whole point of meeting is to really look at everything from every angle, get the disagreements out on the table, and let everybody *be heard.* Because what a lot of research has shown to be the source of people's discontent or anger is feeling like they *weren't* heard.

That's a totally natural response, isn't it? If we feel like, "Oh, you're going to steamroll this over me," it's human nature to say, "Fine, I'm not on board." But if people can get their ideas out, and they feel like everything was hashed out in a healthy environment and we ultimately arrived at the best answer, well then, we've built a meritocracy of *ideas*—not of people, one over the other.

If you cultivate that kind of collegiality, where people are genuinely interested in "What's the best answer here?" then, theoretically at least, everybody will say, "You know what? I was in a different place at the beginning of that discussion. But I'm on board now. I'm willing to commit to this answer, because we all hashed it out together."

The key to getting it from theory to reality lies in ensuring the disagreements are never personal or unfair. Attack and debate an idea or a strategy or an implementation plan, but never a person.

Because that kind of tension is unhealthy for everyone.

HIGH-MAINTENANCE PEOPLE? NOT HERE

SOMETHING I'VE LEARNED OVER time, as I suspect most leaders of start-ups have, is that there are things you do as a fellow human for the other humans and things you scrupulously avoid doing because you've purposely hired other people to do them for you, so you can focus on more complex things.

An example of the latter is booking travel. As discussed more fully in the chapter "Delegation," a leader who spends time doing that is, for one reason or another (none of them good), avoiding the much more important work only they can do (not to mention doing the job of someone else whose job description clearly lists "booking executive travel" among their core functions).

An example of something you can do for the other humans is making coffee.

My cofounder Kevin makes a killer pot of java. Once, soon after we'd hired an exec away from a very large, highly respected tech firm (which shall remain nameless), the new guy arrived for an early morning meeting to find Kevin in the conference room, making coffee.

When we're adding people to our team, whether leaders or players, I have my radar up for high-maintenance people.

"Kevin," he said, "why are you doing that?"

Kevin looked a little perplexed, then said, "Well, I was the first one here. And I figured some of us would want coffee."

Many years later, Harry is still with us and still tells that story.

Where he'd come from, the leaders sat around and waited for the staff to come in and make coffee. Call me indelicate, but there are only two words for that: *high maintenance.*

So when we're adding people to our team, whether leaders or players, I have my radar up for high-maintenance people. People who walk past a piece of trash on the floor because they assume someone else will pick it up. People who don't say thank you to the person who helped them find the right conference room. People who are dismissive to the server at the restaurant.

Because, as I've said to a lot of people in my life, we call the Golden Rule golden for a very good reason: if we'd all just treat others the way we'd like to be treated, life would be a lot more pleasant for all of us.

HIRING

IF YOU'RE STARTING (OR restarting) a company or team, I can't overstate the value of thinking about it like a construction project. You're laying a foundation. Everything that follows will rest on it.

That's why the first twenty-five to fifty people you hire are critical. You can't even *get* to the goal of leading and growing a company without a core group of people who are capable and competent. But with those initial hires, one thing matters even more: that they embrace *your vision and values*.

Your vision enunciates your core beliefs—the reasons you started the company. Your values define the way you want it to operate. It is therefore imperative that your core team is fully on board with your vision and values. If not, it becomes difficult—very quickly—to reinforce and build your vision and values into the touchstone for all your company does.

These first hires will do nothing short of determining your company's *culture*. That is such a loaded word in today's business environment that I've dedicated a separate chapter to defining and understanding what culture is—and isn't.

But here, I want to make clear how profoundly your first hires

You want people who are super-competent but also hungry, reasonably humble, and nice to work with.

influence your organization's long-term success and to provide some thoughts on how to hire well.

People who, for lack of a better word, "fit" your vision will be self-motivated to find *more* people who fit, because they'll want to work with like-minded people.

In a terrific book called *The Ideal Team Player*, Patrick Lencioni spins a fable about the three qualities the best employees share: they're hungry, humble, and smart. We'll explore the interplay of these in just a minute.

First, know this: pretty much every prospective employee you interview will have been forced, at some point, to work with very capable people who also happened to be *real jerks*. That's one of two guardrails I use in hiring people: no "smart jerks." Because no matter how smart a person might be, the negatives of their jerk persona will supersede the positives of their intelligence. Soon their mere presence will become intolerable. Nobody wants that.

You want people who are supercompetent but also hungry, reasonably humble, and nice to work with.

That said, my other guardrail is avoiding folks who are really nice but not terribly competent. I'm happy to have someone like that greet me at the grocery store or hand me a burger at the drive-through window—I'm just not sure I want them working at my company.

Which brings me back to Lencioni and his three key traits: hungry, humble, and smart. An abundance of any one of these, without enough of the other two to balance it, spells trouble.

It's pretty obvious that people who are nice to be around but don't have the mental acuity and/or hunger to drive initiatives are not optimal hires. Far less obvious, however, is the just-as-dangerous and far-more-common practice of targeting smart people with little regard for their hunger or humility.

Though we're naturally attracted to smart people as prospective hires, hiring IQ without considering emotional intelligence can be as bad as bringing in a pleasant person who lacks hunger or mental acuity.

Let's dive into this a little more deeply.

In my industry, nearly everyone has an undergraduate degree. Many have master's degrees or doctorates. But I've learned over time that *smart* isn't enough. Without *hunger* and *humility*, the hallmarks of emotional intelligence, people will struggle to work effectively in teams. And counterintuitive as it might seem, the smarter they are, if they lack emotional intelligence, the *harder* it is for the rest of us to work with them.

The same goes for an overabundance of hunger—or the phrase I prefer, coined by Dr. Carol Dweck, is *growth mind-set*. It refers to people who are always looking to get better, to extend themselves, and to grow. Not necessarily to grow into organizational roles, like becoming a senior manager, but to always get better at the things they do best.

Without that growth mind-set, people can and often do settle into a coasting, complacent mode. Not the kind of employee we want. Not the kind you should want either.

We want people who challenge themselves and who accept challenges from others. Who can hear a colleague's critique and say, "I know he is not attacking me as person; he's trying to help me get better," and who then hold themselves accountable for increasing their expertise.

People like that bring *intelligence*, and in case you missed it, *humility* (the "I still have room to grow" attitude)—both of which balance their *hunger* (or growth mind-set). That's crucial, as anyone who has tried to work with the purely ambitious will quickly confirm.

I think you see where I'm going, but let's bring it full circle with a look at the role intelligence and hunger play in balancing humility.

I always want people who are not afraid of their own competence, who know they're a good developer, a good writer, a good leader. But I want more than that. Whether they were gifted their abilities at birth or developed them over time, alone or with the help of friends and education and experience, I want them *also* to have a strong sense of, "It's not all about me." In fact, that reminds me of the best quote I've ever heard about humility: "Humility isn't thinking less of yourself; it's thinking of yourself less."

That's humility—but again, like hunger and intelligence, *humility* alone will take you only so far. That humble person must also *hunger* to apply their talents to the benefit of something bigger than themselves and must have enough *intelligence* to map and pursue a path for getting there.

I'm a basketball fan, so when I'm thinking about balance, LeBron James is my go-to analogy. Despite being probably the best player of all time, he couldn't bring Cleveland a championship without complementary teammates.

Then there are truly great coaches—Wooden, Popovich, Coach K—who consistently turn singularly talented players into *team* players. They do it by getting guys off their egos. By definition, a team is a group of people working together for success. When ego prevails, that is simply not possible. It's the same with hiring. It's all about balance.

So think like a coach.

Start with a group that strongly supports your vision. Be sure each hire has an appropriate measure of hunger, humility, *and* intelligence. Then trust that they will help attract people who reinforce your vision and values and can refine them into the kind of culture that promotes long-term success: one where everyone plays for each other.

HUMAN RESOURCES? NOT YET

THERE ARE TWO HALVES to Human Resources. (I know, I know, the human half and the resources half, har har. But seriously …)

There's the operational half: benefits and payroll. Very early, we were blessed with an incredibly competent office manager, Amy (who ultimately went on to do much, much more). Amy knew how to make sure we all got paid, that taxes got reported properly, that we all had health insurance—all that stuff. If you're starting out, be sure your office manager (or somebody!) does too.

The other half of HR is what's often called *talent management.*

Here at SailPoint, we didn't hire that kind of HR help until we had over one hundred people. We simply refused to outsource it—whether to an external headhunter or internally, to an HR pro—until both our core and our bench were really deep and solid.

Before we finally hired talent management specialists, HR complaints were referred to Elvis Presley.

(Now would be good a good time to break away for a minute and go read "The Pool Table.")

Okay? Good.

We held out (and let Elvis handle complaints) because it's always been a fundamental value (there's *that word* again) of mine that at less than one hundred people, talent management is *my* job as the CEO. And as the demands of running the business more broadly pulled me away from it, that talent management became our senior leaders' job. And ultimately, we brought on a wonderfully talented head of HR, Abby, who taught us how to scale and professionalize all that stuff.

Many companies contract a headhunter or bring in an HR pro as soon as the core positions surrounding the founders are full, after the first twenty or maybe thirty people. That's a mistake in my view. Think how much deeper your bench and broader the range of its talent will be if senior leadership takes the ball from the founders and does the hiring until there's simply no option but to establish in-house HR recruiting and talent management. Doing this, you've essentially created a *second* core of people who are sure to be aligned with your young organization's values.

That's one of the two rationales that drives this approach, and it's why with Mike at Waveset and Kevin at SailPoint, at least one of us (but often both senior cofounders) did the final interviews of everybody as we built these companies.

The second reason is related to time.

We'd all been around the industry long enough to know people directly or to know people once removed (through a trusted contact) whom we could hire, and outsourcing talent management would just open us to the potential time sink of sifting through five or ten finalists. But the last thing any start-up has is an abundance of time. So though it may seem counterintuitive to be super hands on when time is already at a premium, you actually *save* time by hiring folks you know and trust when you're starting out.

Then, by letting senior management do *its* own hiring too, you assure that the values you and they share become even more deeply engrained.

If you explain all this to your senior management and they complain, don't be cruel.

Just send 'em to Elvis in HR.

IDEA? FEATURE? PRODUCT? BUSINESS?

IF YOU THINK YOU have a great idea for a business, be advised: the ground you must cover in getting from *idea* to *business* is steep, demanding, and—nine times out of ten—near impossible to traverse. Here's why.

An idea on its own is never a business. It's an *idea*, nothing more. The next step in the process is development: turning your idea into a tangible, working *thing*. Let's say you do. You develop it and it works just like you'd hoped. So is it a business now?

Nope. Your thing is actually one of two potential things: a *feature* or a *product*.

Either of these may—or may not—support a business at some point down the road. Much, *much* further down the road. That's not to minimize the achievement of turning your idea into a tangible working thing. It was a lot of work. But to become a *business*, there's still a ton of work ahead of you, and that's *if* your feature or product can *birth and support* a business *at all*.

The huge majority, I'm sorry to say, can't.

Now maybe you're thinking, "Mark! Sheesh! Didn't I see somewhere in this book that you're a *mentor* to entrepreneurs? How the heck is all this *supporting my dream* of disrupting markets? It sounds like the opposite, like you're trying to discourage me!"

If so, I apologize. Let me assure you, nothing could be further from the truth.

THE BOWLING PIN ANALOGY

Before we launched Waveset, I sat in as an adviser to a VC firm. Over that time, I heard all kinds of pitches for all kinds of ideas, features, products, and businesses—and I began to notice what I eventually dubbed the Bowling Pin Analogy.

Almost without exception, people pitching us could describe only one of two things with great clarity: their initial idea—which I took to calling the *headpin*, the first one at the other end of the bowling alley—or their idea's *effect* on humankind once everybody was using it, which I called the *other nine pins*.

Remember, success means knocking down *all ten*.

When someone could describe only the headpin, our reaction was pretty standard: "That sounds interesting. It's a nice idea. But it doesn't sound like something that will ever get big enough, in terms of market opportunity, to go much beyond the idea or feature stage. Have you thought beyond that?"

Invariably, we'd get a blank stare—and then, "No, I just had this idea."

Then there were the people who could describe with great clarity how life would be fundamentally altered thanks to their app or innovation or whatever it was.

"Someday, when everybody has my app, when thousands of

businesses or millions of people are using it, we will be the next (fill in the blank with one of the greatest ten tech companies ever), I will be famous, and we'll all be rich."

But for the life of them, they couldn't tell us how they planned to take out the *headpin*, or even the next two. "We get it," we'd say. "And you're right; it has the potential to impact thousands, or tens of thousands, or even millions of people, because we'll all be reliant on this someday. A true disruption, turning markets on their heads. But how are you going to get it from *here* to there?"

The brave ones would say, "That's why I'm here. I'm pretty sure I can describe what it takes to knock down the next few pins, and I have at least a vague idea of what it will take to knock down the rest. But I'm sure of one thing: it's going to take money I don't have." But only the exceptions—the ones we ultimately funded—had thought things through all the way and could outline *how they'd spend it*.

Shazam is a great example of a *headpin* idea. It's supercool: play even a snippet of a song, and the app identifies it. Impressive. Lots of technology behind it.

Shazam's founders tried hard to turn their idea into a business, and in the end, they shared a tidy sum upon its sale to Apple. Still, the product stage was as far as they got. Shazam was something an established company could sell but not the kind of foundation upon which a company can stand—proving the *headpin* piece of the Bowling Pin Analogy: even the slickest *product* does not necessarily a *business* make.

Which brings me to the *other* nine pins.

When someone pitched us a world-changing-once-everybody-is-using-it-type venture without knowing where they'd even start, we'd often advise them to do some primary and secondary market research to try to figure it out and then come back to us.

Ideas of this ilk leverage what's known as the *network effect*: the more people are using it, the more popular it becomes. A great example of a company launched based on network effect—beyond the obvious one, Facebook—is LinkedIn.

Like many, when I first heard about LinkedIn in the early days, I thought, "I don't *need* this. I know the people I need to know, and I don't need a whole bunch of other people finding me who I don't know and don't know me. What's the point?"

Like everyone else, I sure found out.

LinkedIn successfully traversed the difficult terrain from *idea* to *business*. Even if Microsoft hadn't purchased it, it would likely be doing just fine without them, thank you very much.

FINDING THE "POCKET"

Professional bowlers know how to get strikes: by making contact with the pins in what is known as the *pocket*. So they work on curving the ball into that gap, located between the headpin and the next pin back. This gives the ball, tracking through the other pins, the highest likelihood of taking them all down.

As an entrepreneur, your job is to find that "pocket," which means determining how far an idea can really go. Doing that requires stopping for a moment and asking yourself, "Is this *just* an idea or maybe a feature at best? Or is it a product—and if so, could it actually become (and sustain) a business?"

There is no wrong answer; each of these has value. But understanding the true potential of any idea is the first crucial step in making it a reality.

JAZZ

HAVE YOU EVER THOUGHT of your company as a group of musicians?

It's a common metaphor, but there are a couple of very different ways to think about it. Specifically, orchestras versus jazz combos.

In another chapter, I compare the role of CEO to that of an orchestra's conductor, and I think that holds in the broadest sense. But when it comes to how the business world increasingly works today, I must give props to Max De Pree's wonderful book, *Leadership Jazz*.

Orchestral performance is nothing if not structured. The goal is to take an ultranotated script in the form of sheet music, written specifically for the orchestra's various sections, and play it *exactly as* notated without deviation, as perfectly as possible.

But as De Pree says, we don't want to try to educate the whole world on being musicians.

The orchestral model is measured—literally, orchestrated. Everybody has their orders, and the task is to execute.

But jazz says, "Here's the fundamental structure of the music. Let's see where we can take it."

Both approaches have their value and their place; it's not an

If you want to limit your company's scope right out of the gate, nothing will do that quite so efficiently as trying to orchestrate (read: control) every move it makes.

either-or thing. Well-structured business operations feel more like orchestras, playing set pieces of music in a big, general sense. But even inside such operations, and particularly in start-ups—*any*time you're doing an innovative new thing, in fact—it feels more like jazz: individual players chase down their ideas within a looser structure, because everyone is still figuring out what that structure is capable of supporting.

If you want to limit your company's scope right out of the gate, nothing will do that quite so efficiently as trying to orchestrate (read: control) every move it makes. But if you want to explore the boundaries of what it might do and where it might go, a jazz mind-set—in both you and everyone on the team—is the one to shoot for.

The very *nature* of innovation *requires* improvisation.

JOB
(VERSUS PASSION)

ELSEWHERE I TALK ABOUT the need to get the order of things right. The most crucial place for doing that, in my book (and this *is*, after all, my book!) is at the beginning of a venture.

Too many new companies begin with their vision or their mission. If they'd instead focus first on their values, the others would follow (see "Values, *Then* Vision"). But does this apply to individuals?

I think the answer is yes, but without a strong idea of the how, you risk winding up at one of two extremes: slogging it out in a job you hate or searching in vain for the *perfect* situation.

The literature on work cultures is filled with stories of life-sapping jobs. It's totally possible to spin lug nuts onto passenger-side front wheels eight hours a day for ten years, as people did at the beginning of the Industrial Revolution and Henry Ford's mass production system—but who *wants* to do that? I know, I know—it takes all kinds, and maybe there are those who can really get into their own heads and make a meditation of impact wrenching those suckers on all day for years on end. But does anyone actually *aspire* to it? And

Too many new companies begin with their vision or their mission. If they'd instead focus first on their values, the others would follow.

more important, in this day and age, aren't we past working for the soulless behemoth that treats you like a cog in a machine?

I sure hope so. The counsel most offered these days is to, at minimum, *like* whatever you do, and better yet, go find a job you're passionate about. We'll probably never get to a place where everyone is doing something they love all their life and being paid handsomely to do it; some people have poorer access to education or are geographically removed from the centers of particular types of commerce that interest them, or whatever the case may be.

And sometimes, no matter how well educated or perfectly located or even totally motivated you may be, you're going to have to do work that is not as fulfilling as you might like. This is the fulcrum on which the whole question of job versus passion is—*must be*—balanced.

A lot of young, smart, passionate people sincerely believe they're going to find a job they absolutely adore, every day, all day, and that their lives will be joy filled. If you're one of them—well, (1) you're probably not reading this book, but (2) uh, no.

We call it *work* for a reason. It's hard. It's not play. It's certainly not all pleasure. It's all about problems and solving them—generally, by the way—in the context of a team. And the fulfillment, the joy, comes from doing so.

That's not to say the process has to be drudgery, but if you're thinking it's all coffee and donuts (or if you're in Texas, breakfast tacos … okay, I'm saddling this with my very specific ideas about joy—sorry), you're going to be disappointed.

Sitting back in his dorm room doing the initial work that would eventually become Facebook, I am very confident that Mark Zuckerberg was having fun. But look at him now. Even with wealth beyond his wildest dreams, he has every government—in the free world, at least—breathing down his neck, and on any given day, no small number of unhappy users. Yes, he can insulate himself from these negatives—up to a point. But in the end, Facebook *is* Mark Zuckerberg. And a *whole lot of hard work.*

And *that's* where passion comes in.

Without it, do you think Zuck would go on? Or that he would have even come this far?

There was a point at which Facebook *became work* for Mark Zuckerberg. Maybe it was while he was still in his dorm room. Maybe when it first began to grow beyond what he imagined to be its bounds. Maybe later. But whenever it first dawned on him that he'd created something with the potential to completely shift the way people connect with each other, it's very likely his next question was, "Am I really up for this?" And no matter what you may think of Facebook or Mark Zuckerberg, this much we know: he answered yes.

For me, this is where the rubber meets the road, and though I hate to say it, I see way too many young people expecting to find something that gives them great joy and great passion all day, every day. Then, upon realizing that the job they have can't do that, quitting and continuing what, I promise, will be a never-ending quest.

Here's why.

Accepting that life itself *is* hard work is difficult. It's a fact we all face sooner or later, and the sooner the better. But what matters is how we *respond.*

We can choose to do the hard work of understanding ourselves. Or not.

There is nothing wrong with trying on different jobs and different work contexts. There is plenty wrong with thinking that you'll find one that is all sunshine and lollipops.

So before you start exploring, at least figure out what you love.

What you care enough about that when the challenges come—because they will—you'll be undeterred. That takes real knowledge of yourself, validated by others. Don't be self-deluded. Let others validate that you're good at what you think you're good at, and have the courage and integrity to hear those who tell you what you're not good at.

At the same time, look for things that stir your passion, because as a rule, those are the things we humans tend to master. It would have been near impossible for Mark Zuckerberg to create a whole new kind of social network if he didn't care passionately about *creating social networks*!

So by all means, work hard on identifying and cultivating and learning, backward and forward, every aspect of your passion—but be realistic. Work simply is not all fun all the time. And the more you avoid the things that don't initially feel fun or fulfilling, the more frustrated you will become. Because following your passion means experiencing it fully—the good and the bad—and without an understanding of the bad, how can you make it *even better*?

KINDNESS

SOMETIMES IN A MEETING, I'll get up to get a Coke, and I'll ask the junior person sitting next to me if I can grab them a drink. And they're stunned.

"Oh, you're going to get *me* a drink?"

"Well … yeah. I'm going to the fridge to get a drink. I'll get you a drink too." And I'm thinking, *Did you think I'd delegate getting you a drink to my executive assistant?*

I mean, I get it—there's a hierarchy in business. But it must never preclude basic kindness.

If, in your mind, you ever get too important to get a younger teammate a Coke—someone who's exactly where you were thirty years ago, just trying to figure things out—you've become too important for your own good.

And way too important for your company's good.

KNOWLEDGE VERSUS WISDOM

SOMEONE ONCE SAID, "NEVER confuse one year of experience repeated thirty times with thirty years of experience."

There's a genuine danger, one I see play out too often, when people seem to think that simply because they've read something or understand a given concept, they now know all there is to know about it. Not so.

There is a difference between knowledge and *applied* knowledge, and the difference is wisdom.

For example, at various points in this book, I share the insights of others whose work has influenced me. (I also list them on the resources page.) But just as this would not be *my* book if it did not share *my* experience-based take on things, merely understanding a concept does not imbue one with genuine wisdom about it.

Wisdom *rests upon* understanding and is won, hard, through *experience*—over time and in a variety of real-world circumstances. No Quora discussion, Reddit feed, or Instructable video—or this book—can change that. And when you've learned to filter the

There is a difference between knowledge and applied knowledge, and the difference is wisdom.

knowledge you're acquiring through the prism of experience so that it turns into true wisdom, you often find that there are actually shockingly few beliefs that become truly critical to how you live your life.

Dr. Matt Cassidy, a pastor and a buddy of mine, puts it another way: "The older I get, the fewer convictions I have—and the stronger I hold on to those I know to be true."

LEAD BY EXAMPLE

I DID MY FIRST start-up, Waveset Technologies, in 2000—the heady days just before the dot-com bubble burst.

Back then, the Herman Miller Aeron chair was *the hot item* in offices. It cost well upward of $1,000, and every Silicon Valley start-up decided it had to have one—for *every employee.*

Not us. (*See* "Bring Your Own Chair.")

The Aeron chair became symbolic of an ethos where start-ups seemed more interested in having prime office space and tricked-out offices than in discerning between viable and cockamamie business ideas.

At Waveset, and later at what would become SailPoint, my cofounders and I established the practice of sharing an office for as long as we could. And those office spaces purposely were not in spaces that *anyone* would consider supercool. Nor were their furnishings, chairs or otherwise.

We believed then (and still do) that this sent a very strong message right out of the gate: "This is a start-up. Don't get wrapped up in concerns like the quality of your desk or your office or the view from your window—if you even *have* a window."

Early on, it's crucial to have people who understand the mission and are committed to achieving a successful outcome.

When the tech bubble finally burst, other new companies fell like dominoes.

But not us. I like to think that was due in no small part to our frugal approach.

Early on, it's crucial to have people who understand the mission and are committed to achieving a successful outcome. Cushier offices may ultimately be a *result* of doing so, but they're not what make success possible.

SailPoint newbies who walked into the office I shared with my cofounder immediately got that message. The few who didn't were bound to get it soon enough from one of their colleagues: "Really, you're going to complain about *your* office? Have you *seen* Mark's and Kevin's?"

This is a textbook example of *leading* by example—something we hear a lot about but see much less frequently. So if you say it, show you mean it: Don't take a limo; rent a cheap car. Don't fly first class; fly coach.

Equally important: understand that frugality applied to the *wrong* situation can be as dangerous as extravagance when it's misapplied. (*See* "Wrong Time for the Red-Eye.")

LIFE, HAVING A

The unexamined life is not worth living.

—*Socrates*

IF YOU TRY TO achieve at a high level in the work environment at a pace that just doesn't allow you to have a life, you will pay a price.

It's a price many have paid before you. The question, which I explore more deeply elsewhere (*see* "Balance, Life-Work"), is whether you can become adept at knowing when to adjust your pace. And that, as the quote atop this chapter suggests, requires constant examination.

You can sprint. When you're in a crunch, when there's a crisis, you'll have to. But if you don't even that out—or worse, fail to recognize that there is no such thing as a daily crisis—you're going to wake up one day with no friends, no family, no fun.

It's parallel, to me, with the notion of giving back. I've said that giving back to the communities in which our companies operate needs to be a value we instill from day one, rather than a goal or something we'll do once we've made it.

Having a life is the same. You can't put in ten or twenty or thirty years of hard labor and realistically expect to one day flip the work switch off and the *life* switch on. A life is something you build every day, and like everything else, it takes *effort*. It means *thinking about* the dimensions of your life that you care about *beyond* work, beyond career, beyond building a business.

Thought requires time. It might be fifteen minutes of quiet each morning, when you kind of reset your brain; a weekly hour you set aside; or maybe a monthly Tuesday afternoon away from everything. But the idea is the same: to step back, assess, and make sure you're not losing track of life writ large. That you're in balance, or at minimum that you haven't gotten so far out of balance that you can't find your way back.

Put simply, having a life requires thinking regularly about the life you're having.

LOVE

ONE OF THE SCREWY things about English is we have only one word to express intense passion for something, regardless what it is: I *love* spaghetti, I *love* my dog—and, oh, by the way, I *really* love my *wife*!

We have other words, but none captures the intensity quite like *that* one. "I'm *fond of* spaghetti." Hmmm … okay.

So we have this heavy, heavy word—and if we're not using it, folks generally jump to the conclusion that we could like whatever it is we're talking about *more*. So we do use it, even when our actions clearly show that we care plenty.

People who love their dogs, for instance. Think about what *they* sacrifice. Sleep: Rover wants out at 5 a.m. Every. Single. Day. Money: Pets aren't cheap. I have a friend who spends nearly as much boarding his two dogs when the family goes on vacation as he spends on *their own lodging*!

Whether he uses the word or not, trust me: *that's* love.

So what about the work context?

You can say you love your colleagues and your work and your boss, but how do you *show* it?

Elsewhere I talk about brewing coffee when you're the first one

Real love almost always involves sacrifice. Except when you love someone, it doesn't feel like sacrifice at all. It feels like something you want to do.

in, not waiting until a lower-level employee comes in. Or getting a soda for a junior person when you're getting one for yourself. It's the same thing you'd do at home: "Hey, sweetie, I'm headed to the store. Do you need anything?"

Selflessness. Service. Ultimately, humility—putting others before you, and in so doing, putting the whole notion of win-win into practice. In fact, the belief that I should *help* my colleague to win, even when it sometimes costs me something, is what constitutes "love" at work. Because real love almost always involves sacrifice. Except when you love someone, it doesn't feel like sacrifice at all. It feels like something you want to do. It even brings you *joy*, something we don't talk much about in the workplace.

We can win together. I can win. You can win. We all can win *if* we learn how to love each other—even at work.

MANAGER—OR NOT?

DO YOU LIKE TO do work yourself, or do you like to get work done through others?

This, in my opinion, is the fundamental line determining who does and doesn't have management potential. Unfortunately, that's not how most organizations think.

If someone is good at a function, all the organization's energies and hierarchies are geared toward promoting that person—to have them manage a group of people who are doing that same thing, whether or not that person is interested in managing at all.

It's the well-known Peter Principle: people in hierarchical organizations tend to rise through promotion to a respective level of incompetence.

Just think of all the hall-of-fame players from the sports world who have become great coaches or general managers.

Go ahead ... I'm waiting.

Meanwhile, the list of former players who failed spectacularly in those roles is long and still growing—because *doing* is one thing, and *managing* is something else entirely.

So before you think you'd like to manage people, ask yourself

True managers aspire to assemble teams that are so high functioning that, at a minimum, they could function reasonably well for a long time in the manager's absence.

this: "What do I enjoy *most?*"

If you like working through others and helping them achieve success, you might be great in a management role. But if you're hands on, you may find management challenging at best, intolerable at worst. (*See* "Not A Manager—But … ")

It goes further—to what for many is a completely counterintuitive thought: the *best* managers want to *make themselves useless.* True managers aspire to assemble teams that are so high functioning that, at a minimum, they could function reasonably well for a long time in the manager's absence. At the most extreme level, on a truly amazing team, it would theoretically be possible for anyone on the team to take the reins and successfully direct the work for a long time.

But there are flies in the proverbial ointment, little things like personalities and egos. And that's why most people—non-managers—worry that if those around them become so successful that they are no longer needed, they will be in trouble. And so they try to protect their jobs by getting political.

True managers know better. They're the first to take responsibility when criticism surfaces about those they lead or the projects they manage, but they are also quick to reflect praise back to the people who really do the work. They say to themselves, "The best thing I can be as a first-line manager is *no longer needed.* Then I can move up to *second* line, and one of the great people I work with now can take my place." And so on and so forth. And that's how people find themselves getting promoted from managers to VPs and maybe even all the way to CEO.

MARKETING

WHEN YOU'RE BUILDING A business, you're dealing with two primary concerns: building real products and building real cultures. When it comes to marketing, you're working mainly—but not entirely—on the product side.

Similarly, an effective marketing operation has two aspects: input and output.

A lot of companies focus their marketing efforts more (and often entirely) on output, believing that whatever products they create or services they offer, the marketing team will figure out how to position them so the sales team can sell them. That's the objective many companies set for their marketing operations, isn't it? Telling the world about their stuff in a way that entices people to try it out.

These organizations ignore (at worst) or give short shrift (at best) to the *input* aspect of marketing, and doing the input piece right is the only way to guarantee—a strong word, I know—success.

A big clue to this truth can be found right at the beginning of one of the oldest maxims in business. It's known as the "four Ps of marketing" (for product, price, place, and promotion). If any one of these elements of the process is not performed optimally, successful marketing of whatever you are selling becomes *much* more difficult.

And the *very first* item is *product*.

Translation: If your product is optimal, it *should* sell because it's designed to solve real pain points, and competent salespeople should be able to sell it. Simple as that. (You can still mess up even with great products, but I'll leave that topic for a true sales expert, which I am not.)

So how do we develop *optimal products*? And what does *input* have to do with it?

The answer to both questions is *market research*.

Market research, in my opinion, is *the essential function* of the marketing role. Without undertaking it long before a product gets to the concept stage (let alone into production), you might as well buy a lottery ticket—because your odds of developing a successful product or service or whatever it is are approximately as good. And market research is an input function: your company, getting input.

Still, many companies go right on to create marketing departments focused mainly on output. They hire writers and graphics folks and PR people who produce and deliver slick marketing materials and who chat up their products—products based on little more than the gut feeling of one or more of the organization's important people, that "This thing can't miss!" In such organizations, market research never even gets a seat at the product development table, although its rightful seat in *any* organization is at the *head* of that table.

When you do product development without input from prospective customers, you not only expend your efforts on something they may not want. You also make each of the remaining three Ps of marketing (price, place, promotion) *even more* difficult. How can you know what *price* the market will bear if you're not *listening* to it? Or where to *place* your new product so the market will *discover* it?

Once you've created a product people don't want, priced it wrong, and put it in the wrong places, trust me—all the *promotion* in the world won't sell it.

Sadly, Bill had never heard of the four P's.

Bill, the lead engineer at XYZ company, was eating a banana one day on his break and got a notion for a product he thought would change the world: an automatic banana peeler. "How *cool* would *that* be?" Bill asked a few colleagues in the break room. "Any size banana, this thing would pull it off of the bunch, sense its ripeness, peel it with the appropriate force so as not to bruise it, and present it to the waiting recipient!"

"Whoa," one guy responded. "That's, like, as cool as a food replicator on *Star Trek*. Well, almost as cool. But pretty cool, for sure!" Bill's other coworkers nodded in agreement, then exchanged glances that said, "Can we go back to eating now?"

But it was all the encouragement Bill needed. Soon he was spending his free time in his basement, perfecting the design. He went back to the drawing board repeatedly, as his brainchild mangled bunch after bunch—but God bless him, he kept plugging away.

Ten years passed, and one morning, Bill greeted his spouse, Mary, at the breakfast table. In the middle sat a perfectly ripened bunch of bananas. Next to it was Bill's surprisingly small, elegant—gorgeous, really—contraption: a picture of both simplicity and high-tech chic. "You know the drill, honey," Bill said.

Rolling her eyes—she'd clearly done this many times before— Mary dutifully said, "Can I have a banana, please?" holding out her hand in a too-perfunctory way.

The machine whirred into graceful action. It gently grabbed and separated a fruit from its bunch, flawlessly stripped it of its skin, then swiveled it outward. "Handing" it to Mary, it responded simply in a voice Siri would envy: "My pleasure."

"Wow!" Mary said. "It *finally worked!* *That* was supercool! Amazing! Honey, you are incredible!" She threw her arms around his neck, gave him a big hug, and when she turned to take the banana, stopped, her hand poised a few inches away.

"What is it?" Bill asked.

"Well, I'm just thinking about it … "

"Yes?"

"Can you make it leave the skin half on?"

"What?" Bill asked incredulously. "Why?"

"Well," Mary began, "sometimes when I've been out working in the garden, I come inside for a break and eat a banana."

"Right." Bill says. "And?"

"Well," the love of Bill's life replied, "my hands are dirty."

"So?" Bill coaxed her, not a little impatiently.

"Well, if I could take it by the *skin*, I wouldn't have to worry about washing up first! I could come in, ask for a banana, take it, and get right back to the garden. I mean, don't get me wrong. It's supercool watching your machine peel it, but if my hands are dirty … "

Bill forced a smile and gently nodded. He even managed to say, "Thank you for your input, dear."

He picked up his invention and returned to the basement door. Then he opened it and bounced his brainchild down the stairs.

Product, price, place, promotion.

Bill never got the *first* one right because—like so many other designers and engineers—he convinced himself right at the start that *cool* was enough.

It never is.

People buy products because they solve actual, real-world

problems, yet designers and engineers run around creating solutions before asking themselves—and more critically, *asking others—what* the problem is.

You don't take vitamins for a headache; vitamins won't solve that problem. You take aspirin or some other pain reliever.

Similarly, dreaming up products that don't target a specific problem is pointless and creates more headaches than it relieves.

Yet companies become convinced that, by their very coolness, given products will disrupt markets and change life as we know it; then the companies seemed genuinely amazed when no one buys the products.

People buy products because they solve actual, real-world problems, yet designers and engineers run around creating solutions before asking themselves— and more critically, asking others— what *the problem is.*

Good products *almost sell themselves* ("almost" because depending on the product or the complexity of the buying process, there's often a need for sophisticated selling techniques). They make the *output* piece of the marketing operation the easiest, because if you get the *input* piece right—by finding out what people want (product), what they're willing to pay (price), and where they prefer to buy it (place)—letting them know it's available (promotion) is all that's left. If you have the first three right, it won't take much output to prosper.

People are smart. They quickly recognize when something is a significant improvement to what they're using now and even *more* quickly recognize when something is all sizzle and no steak.

So truly great marketing goes to the market *first*, not last. It asks prospective buyers two simple questions. "Where does it hurt?" and "What will make the pain go away?"

For proof, look no further than the greatest consumer electronics company of all time: Apple.

Think about the market research that had to precede the development of the iPod. At the time, there were other ways to have portable music, most notably the Sony Walkman. But Apple cracked all kinds of codes—from volume to flexibility to size.

Advances like that are not made in a vacuum. They're made by talking to real people, who are tired of wrangling (and mangling) cassette tapes and CDs, changing batteries constantly, and the whole galaxy of issues that made the Walkman—once users were encouraged to be honest about it—a pain in the derriere.

It only took asking them those two simple questions, "Where does it hurt?" and "What will make the pain go away?" And then *listening* to what the market said.

I assume Apple did the same thing with the iPhone. People already had mobile phones—but what if their phones could become fully functional *computers*?

That's another thing good marketing does: it asks, "What if?" and takes the market's answers seriously. It doesn't pretend to know better than the customer; in fact, it is sure that it *never does*.

If you're building products *for your fellow engineers*, you can get close to what that market *likes*. But if you are an engineer building for *nonengineers*, you will often miss what the market *needs*—because what's "cool" to a broader market is simply *what works best*, not what showcases technology, flash, or looks simply *because it can*. If the technology is not applied to a real, stubborn, seemingly intractable need, the broader market simply *will not care*.

So go to the market *first*. Ask what it needs and listen. Then present the challenge to engineers and designers, and don't accept anything from them that doesn't fully resolve the challenge.

Next, return to the market. Test the solution, and take it back to the engineers and designers.

Repeat this process as many times as necessary until the market finally says, "That's it!"

There's a reason the process is called product *development*—not product *creation*. And superior products are developed only when marketing input precedes marketing output.

MARKETS,
LISTENING TO

EVERY COMPANY I'VE BEEN involved with has been different, but there's been one constant at each: the interrelatedness of what, to the casual observer, looks like wildly different arms of the operation.

Sales and engineering. Customer service and purchasing. HR and product development. The areas in each of these seemingly disparate pairings interrelate; they have overlap with each other, *and* to all the areas in the other pairings, though their relatedness is not always obvious. This is true because we're talking about organizations, which are systems.

In any successfully functioning system, each constituent part interacts with each of the other parts, in varying degrees and at various times, in assuring the whole functions effectively. The better they work together, the healthier and more fully the system—or company—operates.

If you asked me to name a *single* function that unifies and holds successful operations together, I'd pick listening to markets. Any company that is not doing so in a strategic, repeatable, consistent way, and applying what it learns, is not going to be around very long.

I discuss the importance of listening to markets throughout this book, but here I want to get into the nuts and bolts: how to actually do it.

* * *

Whether we're talking about a market you already serve or one you want to move into, listening effectively to it can be thought about in terms of vitamins versus aspirin. We all know we should take our vitamins, but many of us are lazy about it. If we skip a day, we don't sweat it too much. We'll take them tomorrow. But when we have a screaming headache, we'll *knock somebody over* on the way to find some Tylenol! Just *make the pain stop*!

This perfectly illustrates a distinction, critical when attempting to learn what customers *really* need, which struggling companies simply don't get. They listen to what people say they'd *like* to have or *think* they need but don't verify that it's something they *must* have—that without it, their work will remain painful in a significant enough way that, when some other company figures out how to make the pain stop, they'll line up to sign up.

If this process of verifying *real* customer needs versus "wants" or "nice to haves" sounds difficult, it is. And the more your product development people think they *already know* what customers need, the tougher it gets. Sound travels quickly. Light speed is blinding. But both move in slow motion compared to the time it takes for a customer to realize they're *not being heard*.

What happens next is worse: the customer realizes they are not being heard because the person they are talking to is certain *they* know more about the customer's pain and how to solve it than the customer does—and the customer simply shuts down. "What's the point?" they think. "I've got better things to do with my time."

In our increasingly tech-centric world, it's a common circumstance. Engineers get cocky. "I know all about tech. I know what people want, so I'll build it for them."

Wrong. And, I might add, *not* exclusive to tech. Since long before the information age dawned, companies have believed they know what's best for their customers—and they and their companies have generally gone to their graves still convinced of it.

HUMILITY—AND "WHERE DOES IT HURT?"

It takes two things to listen to markets effectively: humility and a determination to fully appreciate what is causing customers' pain. That's true whether you're trying to figure out the shortcomings of a competitor's product to move into their market or whether you want to address the pain your own product is causing, so a competitor doesn't do the same thing to you.

Humility means accepting that your target buyer in any market *knows more* about what they're doing than you do—and *always will*. It's something not everyone is capable of; their egos prevent it. You don't want those people working for you (*see* "Hiring").

You want people who are sincere about listening to markets. Who want to listen closely to the people who are living the pain. Who push them for the *real sources* of their pain. And—while you want them to make note of them—people who don't get lost in the things customers say they'd *like* or that would be *nice*, because they know that if they can make the pain stop, those other issues will often melt away.

People with the ability to do this are invaluable and worth finding. They are your key to gaining real insight into the markets you already serve and those you want to.

In early testing, product development folks will ask, "Would it be more helpful if the product did this or if it did that? Or does this *other* idea sound helpful to you?" These questions make sense when you're trying to define what you're building and testing it. But it's not going to help you open new markets or make current frustrated customers happier with your already-rolled-out products.

(Side note: In the world of software-as-a-service products, there is a new advantage available today to companies. It's quite feasible to do "mini-experiments," rolling a new feature or capability into their offering, seeing how people use it (or not), and then tweaking it gradually until they see usage start to accelerate. In other words, the existing product users are helping you validate the importance of new things based simply on observing their behavior online. It's starting to accelerate the pace of acceleration in many, many product areas.)

That takes a whole different approach. You want them to *light up*, to *beat* you up, to get *so emphatic* about what's pushing their buttons, and why, and what an effective solution would look like to them that you fully understand how to make their pain stop. You'll know when it happens. They'll say, "Oh, yeah—that! *That* drives me *crazy*! Why won't it let me *do that*?"

* * *

So I've offered my prescription: the approach and the goal of listening to markets. But how do you actually get in front of the customers who are in pain—be they your own or a competitor's (whose lunch you're hoping to eat)—and what type of people make the best listeners, able to do what I've just described?

MARKET RESEARCH AND LACK OF INVESTMENT

Finding customers who are in pain requires market research, which runs on two tracks: secondary and primary.

You always want to do enough secondary research that you understand the lay of the land before you move to the primary research of sitting down with potential customers. That can mean reading and absorbing and getting a feel for what's happening in the market, if you're looking to expand. If you're in a market already, you probably already know its ebbs and flows, what other vendors are doing, and what solutions others have put out there.

To develop effective solutions, though, you have to get in front of your target customers, and this opens onto the people you want to put in front of them.

One reason companies use market-research firms is specifically because they are not connected to the company. Primary research undertaken by a market-research firm can be effective for both identifying and curing the pain of your own customers and for doing the same with new markets—your competitors' customers.

These firms use surveys, focus groups, and other assessment techniques. My only caution is to assure they've done the secondary research necessary to ask the questions that will push customers to open up about their pain; otherwise, you'll be wasting time and money. They must also carefully target, screen, and vet the participants in their research to make sure they're getting in front of the right people, the ones you're trying to help.

The attraction of using market-research firms is their independence. They have no investment in the products you already sell or those you seek to develop, so they are able to unearth and provide facts that have not been colored by the defensiveness or company

People who don't have a lot of knowledge and experience with a market may not understand its nuances.

advocacy—in other words, baggage—that employees of your company would bring. But it bears repeating: if the researchers are not fully versed in your industry and intimate with the particular issue you seek to resolve for customers, their report may be shallow and disappointing.

Instead, while we have occasionally used independent firms to help us, I prefer to assemble listening teams from within the company, carefully selecting members to assure they understand the mission and have that humble attitude described above. While they may have some investment in the product we are trying to fix or market issue we hope to leverage in opening a new market, it's important that they be truly objective about what they're hearing. That's why it's sometimes helpful to have people who haven't spent their whole lives in the industry; they have "fresh eyes." But it can be tricky. People who don't have a lot of knowledge and experience with a market may not understand its nuances.

There are lots of examples of people who bounced from one market or industry to another with phenomenal results, while others butchered things for good. Lou Gerstner jumped from Nabisco to IBM, and nobody thought a guy who had never been in technology would figure out how to run a giant computer company. But for many years, Gerstner did amazing things at IBM.

Then there's John Sculley, who went from Pepsi to Apple and was a disaster for a decade.

So you have two guys who went from consumer food products to technology with wildly different outcomes. I won't pretend to know why, but I'd bet that their ability—or lack of it—in listening to markets loomed large. You have two people who are trying to listen to and solve problems. If you're new to the market and don't understand all the nuances, that's a problem. But at the same time, it's an opportunity and one that can be applicable here.

If you come in with totally fresh eyes, you can think of the problem in a completely different way.

Tim Brown at IDEO leverages this. He brings really different disciplines into a room, like an architect when he's trying to solve a computer programming issue. Why? Because architects think differently.

So in trying to listen to markets, I think you get a fuller picture when you have a mixture of people. You want some with a deep understanding of the market so you don't miss the nuances.

But for balance, you also want fresh eyes and fresh thinkers, unburdened by the baggage that can make objectivity difficult for those who are more intimate with the market, the company, or both.

NAMES, KNOWING PEOPLE'S

NOTHING IS MORE IMPORTANT to any of us than *who we are*.

I don't know the name of everybody at SailPoint when I see them in the hallway. We grew beyond that possibility a number of years ago. There are (purportedly) people who can remember the name of everyone they've ever met.

I'm not one of them.

But I *can* learn the names of the people I see every day. Just by taking the time to do that, to learn the front desk gal or guy's name or the janitor's name or the security guard's name, I send the message that I understand the truth of this chapter's first sentence.

You can do that too. You should.

Because—like getting a soda for that junior person sitting with you in a meeting—*it matters*.

NARCISSISM

SEE "DONNA, PRIMA."

NOT A MANAGER–
BUT ...

ELSEWHERE I PROVIDE MY best clues for figuring out if someone is a manager (*see* "Manager—or Not?") and how the organizational charts of most companies are set up to motivate employees to work into management roles. The motivators, of course, being money and prestige.

This would be fine if it actually worked. It doesn't.

If it did, we wouldn't get managers who grab the wheel when something isn't happening as efficiently as they'd like, who claim credit for the successes of those they manage, and who shift blame for their own failures onto them.

Tech companies have been notably good at creating an alternative to the corporate ladder. On what's often referred to as the *technical ladder*, it's possible to be a very well-paid, senior-level person who is *not* a manager. The chief technical officer (CTO) at many companies doesn't really "manage" any people and has no or few direct reports. Still, they are superinfluential.

I believe all organizations can take a lesson from tech on this count. But to work, it has to come from and be vigorously supported in the executive suite: creating opportunities for great technical (i.e., skilled) people who do not want to be or should not be managers, to stay with you, make lots of money, and be recognized as key contributors to the organization's success.

There are many great reasons for doing this, not least the one that happens to also be the most pragmatic: if you don't recognize and pay these people for what they do, someone else will.

Technical positions exist in every field—not just technology. Maybe you run an auto repair business. There is going to be one mechanic that all the others go to with problems they just can't figure out, because they know he or she can. That person isn't a manager—but maybe they're the chief mechanic, or senior mechanic, or what have you. They make you a lot of money by mentoring others: helping them avoid mistakes and find the most efficient approaches to challenges. That is very different from directing (managing) them.

Think instead about rewarding the people in your organization whose outsized impact and competence earn them management-level compensation.

The minute you turn that guy or gal into a manager and give them responsibility for the flow of work, the quality of work, whatever it may be, you change them and every interaction they have with the other mechanics. And if they really love their work, they're unlikely to see those changes as being for the better.

We see this too in white-collar settings. In an early-stage company, it is just fine (excellent, in fact) if the top salesperson makes a million bucks when the CEO is making a quarter of a million. *That's what you want.*

So why not carry that ethos through? Why confuse and distract people—people who are great at what they do, and as happy as pigs in mud doing it—with the brass ring of management?

Think instead about rewarding the people in your organization whose outsized impact and competence earn them management-level compensation.

When you remove the pressure on people to become something they are not—managers—and replace it with the possibility, available to anyone, of enjoying the status, respect, and success they would have as a manager and give them the opportunity to do that by simply doing what they love, you enrich not just their work experience but the culture of the whole organization.

OVERBEARING UNDERPERFORMERS

I'VE TALKED ABOUT THE dangers of prima donnas, ridiculously talented people with massive egos. (*See* "Donna, Prima.")

Another challenge is the person who's constantly telling you how great they are but doesn't produce results backing up their claims.

I can (barely but seldom) tolerate prima donnas for a little while, because I can at least acknowledge their obvious talent. I don't like the ego, but the skill is undeniable.

But when someone isn't even doing a good job and is fixated on telling me how great

When an underperformer extolls his or her own virtues, it's beyond cocky; grating pretty much captures it.

they are, that's a lot harder to accept. Indeed, in a healthy company, it's pretty much impossible.

In both cases it's an ego problem. In the case of the supertalented person, at least there's some justification.

When an underperformer extolls his or her own virtues, it's beyond cocky; grating pretty much captures it. I'm no fan of cockiness (*see* "Donna, Prima"), but when it's coupled with poor performance, I've found exactly one elegant solution: convincing them to take their incredible talents elsewhere.

Ideally, a competitor.

PARTNERS: PUNCH ABOVE YOUR WEIGHT CLASS

I'M A TECHNOLOGY GUY, and I love (most of) what technology has brought us. But the word *innovation* has become pretty much synonymous with electronic technology. That's really too bad.

Humankind has been innovating all along. Foundational advances that paved the way to how we innovate today and even how we *think* about innovation today—from Gutenberg to Edison to Ford—had nothing to do with electronics.

Still, the ubiquity of the idea that all of today's innovation can be traced to tech persists, probably because tech innovations make the most noise in the marketplace.

This chapter is centered on B2B partnering, but I've prefaced my thoughts on it around innovation, because a key truth of the B2B world is true in consumer markets as well: to grow and prosper, companies need to offer something nobody else does. Whomever you're selling to, your innovation—or at minimum, your overall business proposition—must be different (in a word, better) than what is already available from established players, or you're never going to win. Because customers, whether B2B or end users, are *smart*. They'll think, "This is basically the same thing I can already get, and I already know that platform [or company, or product]. They're big, they're established, and I've already got experience with their product [or a contract with them in the B2B world]."

You'll never win.

But if you have a *true innovation*—tech or otherwise, B2B or consumer—one of the best ways to grow it is to align with big, established companies whose products and services people already know.

I call this punching above your weight, and doing it makes even the smallest start-up feel immediately bigger, more vibrant, and more *vital*.

In SailPoint's case (and we are a B2B company), it meant working with players like Accenture, Deloitte, EY, KPMG, and PwC, big firms who would play big roles in our go to market. When we'd pitch to a Fortune 500 shop with someone from one of these firms at our side, it made an impression. At minimum, the prospect firm would think, "Okay, these guys must be on to something. This guy from an industry giant is telling me to consider them."

To get into the ring against big players, you have to look like you're in their league and able to fight with them. That willingness to punch above your weight is often where the wheat is separated from the chaff. (Threshing machines—totally nonelectronic innovations. Just sayin'.)

True entrepreneurs are not intimidated by big firms. They understand that such firms are often as interested in working with start-ups as the start-up is in partnering with them. Leading firms stay that way by finding new, emerging, cool technologies that can help their client companies.

It's a thin line, however, between being unintimidated by big-name companies and coming off as cocky. Confidence is fine; cockiness won't fly. I've seen a number of young companies get thrown out on their ear because they come in with the attitude of, "Hey, man, I'm here to change your universe."

The next thing they hear is, "What are you talking about? I've been doing this since before you were born."

From there, the walk to the parking lot feels like a death march.

PAY IT FORWARD

IF YOU'VE BEEN FORTUNATE—BLESSED with some level of success in your career, particularly as an entrepreneur—I hope that you feel compelled to get out there and help the next generation of entrepreneurs.

That said, it's critical to know specifically *where* your strengths lie and to try to leverage them to the benefit of others. Don't be lulled into believing what I'll call, for lack of a more fitting cliché (!), your own PR. By which I mean the thought that maybe you've achieved a lot of what you have single handedly. You haven't.

None of us has.

There are things you are good at, to be sure. The key is *knowing* what you're good at and letting others do what *they're* good at. That's a key message I try to deliver to those I mentor, and it's true no matter the stage of maturity at which your company now sits.

I've seen the truth in this not just at work but in mentoring itself. At some point—probably around the time we IPOed SailPoint—I was forced to recognize that my experience as a founder, and over time as being more of a big picture guy, had rendered a lot of my thoughts pretty unrelatable to incubating companies or those at a superearly stage.

It's critical to know specifically where your strengths lie and to try to leverage them to the benefit of others.

Today I feel more valuable in some important ways to midstage entrepreneurs who have gotten some traction and are confronted with figuring out how to scale. That can happen only after the company shows it can figure things out, so it is really the next step, and it is a very different one.

Meanwhile, my business partner and cofounder at SailPoint, Kevin, is the expert at helping people figure out the efficacy of their prescription—whether they have the *right* pain reliever or not (*see* "Marketing"). Nobody is better at listening to markets describe their pains and pushing companies to constantly develop the right treatments.

I totally get that the right prescription is going to create demand, but my thing is looking at how to scale up to meet it: how to attract and hire the right teammates who can build out a culture and a management approach that will not only survive but enhance the company's growth process.

There's a broader point here: figuring out, when you've been gifted with some level of success, the appropriate ways to pay that back—and forward.

Some people see paying it forward as spending a bunch of time in the nonprofit community or social ventures. I think both worlds, profit and nonprofit, are acceptable avenues for giving back. If you can spend some of your time helping next-gen business entrepreneurs and some in whatever charitable cause you naturally gravitate to—education, children in need, whatever it may be—that's great.

Broadening it even more, it's really about how you spend your free time.

To me, running around the world and living a largely hedonistic lifestyle doesn't really benefit anybody. When you have a lot of success, I think some amount of enjoying what you've built or accumulated in life is fine; I just don't think it's what we're here for.

One, certainly two generations back, you worked hard at a job, then you stopped working—and *voila!*—you were retired. I think for most of my generation and those into the foreseeable future, somewhere between fifty and sixty-five we might think, sure, we'd love to maybe dial it back a little, create a different mix. But the idea of *doing nothing* related to work just doesn't get it. Playing golf every day of the week in my sixties doesn't even sound fun; it sounds terrible. (Although, maybe if I *shot* every day in the sixties, I'd feel differently!)

In another chapter (*see* "Life-Work Balance"), I talk about life never being in perfect balance 24/7 and illustrate it with a pie chart. I think increasingly more people see the "work" slice never going completely away, but I can totally see it changing labels to "paying it forward." Whether that's mentoring younger entrepreneurs or bringing your expertise to nonprofits or a combination of both, terrific. It doesn't need to be forty hours a week, but it shouldn't be zero either.

I meet young entrepreneurs all the time whose goal is making a pile of money and retiring in their thirties. And I'll say, "Really? What are you going to do with all that time?" Usually, I get a blank stare. Or they might say they want to travel around the world or play a lot of golf. "Really?" Frankly, it doesn't take much more dialogue to get them to rethink whether they'll really be all that satisfied doing that for another *fifty years*. Point made.

Do they really think they'll stay healthy and vibrant and able to do things if they're just goofing off or pursuing hobbies? Few hobbies are as fulfilling as sharing our experiences with those coming up behind us and helping them succeed—and I believe part of that is maturing into a giving mind-set.

But okay, let's say you go hard after golf—or better yet, I do. We've already established that I'm not in the subpar realm. But even if I went after it day after day, *I'm working.* Maybe I'd eventually get down to a two handicap, but at some point (probably much sooner than later), I'd level off and would need to put in ten *more* hours *a week* just to get another *shot or two* off my number. And for what? Do I really (*seriously!*) believe I'm going to—what, *play on the tour?* Become a local hustler?

Thanks to having some success in business, I'm going to eventually ask myself, "Is this giving me a good ROI?"

Instead, I view retirement as a line that you symbolically approach but never quite reach.

On a continuum, I feel like in your forties, as a successful entrepreneur, you can be helping twenty-somethings. But being a continuum—well, it continues, doesn't it?—there's always a generation or even two below you to which you can be providing counsel and help.

I believe successful businesspeople have a responsibility to do that, and it doesn't go away just because you wake up one morning and you're *x* years old.

POOL TABLE, THE

THOSE OF US WHO cofounded Waveset Technologies (the predecessor company to SailPoint) were at Tivoli, which became part of IBM. Not long afterward, Tivoli bought a company in Indianapolis, and one of our eventual Waveset founders, Mike, had a pool table he wasn't using, so he offered it to the folks in Indy. All they had to do was come to Austin and get it, and they did.

Two years later, we were all ready to strike out on our own and form Waveset. But now IBM had this pool table. *Our* pool table. In Indianapolis.

Down in Austin, we wanted it back. It was symbolic of our life as a brand-new start-up. So we headed to Indy to rescue the pool table—four guys who, at that point, weren't kids anymore. We *had* kids. Nonetheless, we went for it—ROAD TRIP! And totally gave in to the fun of it.

That, of course, included going to Graceland—Memphis was on the way. But we didn't think about trivial things like our arrival time. The picture of all of us—outside the gates—is time-stamped 11 p.m. But all was not lost in our attempt to pay homage to Elvis; we bought a life-size stand-up cardboard version of him in his prime at a souvenir shop, loaded him up, and kept rolling.

On to Indy. We loaded the pool table, turned the truck around, and headed home.

In the end, the pool table kept us entertained throughout Waveset's start-up and eventual acquisition. And as it turned out, so did Elvis.

We set up our full-size cutout of the king of rock and roll in the corner of our shared office. Whenever an employee walked in with a complaint, we'd send them to our HR guy over in the corner. We knew he'd accord their issue the kind of tight-lipped confidentiality you want in an HR pro.

Best of all, neither Elvis nor the pool table has left the building. Both are now happily ensconced at SailPoint.

PRIORITIES, SETTING

YOU'LL NEVER BE TAKEN seriously as a leader if you don't do the things leaders do. And leaders do important things like defining strategy, ensuring the right people are in the right seats on the bus (to quote Jim Collins), and making sure the whole team is aligned through regular, effective communication. In fact, many of these tasks are things that only the leader can do. But one of the most important things leaders do is face risks and challenges in the business head-on. The longer you wait to address such priorities, the greater the threat they'll pose.

Whether you lead a department, a division, or the whole shootin' match (just so I don't get in trouble with the antigun crowd, that's old-time Texan for "the whole company"), you will regularly face such challenges. Unchecked, they can threaten at minimum the smooth functioning of your operation—and at worst its very existence. Leaders recognize these challenges early and, by dealing with them as they arise, never allow them to become existential threats.

We humans tend to prioritize things based on their relative urgency. That's not an awful way to go as a leader, but better still is classifying tasks into one of three types: things we must do, things

The list of things leaders must do is always long. Provided you are doing them, it's okay to dip into stuff you like to do, used to do, or simply can do.

we like to do, and things we can do. In general, if something falls into one of the latter two categories, I try my best to entrust it to somebody else.

"Wait," you may be thinking, "does that mean you never do anything you like to do or that you can do?"

Not at all. It just means knowing the difference between being effective as a leader and—to put it bluntly—wasting my time. That said, not all noncritical tasks are time wasters.

In the chapter "Delegation," I mention time along with inclination and lack of trust as often driving leaders to take on things that could or should be done by others.

But that responsibility to consistently take up challenges that only we, by virtue of our positions, must do *includes* doing comparatively menial things because it *reminds those we lead* that we actually *live* the servant-leader model, not just talk about it.

I can't seriously expect people to be servant-leaders if I don't walk the talk. I can't say, "Hey, none of us is too good to do stuff," then use my position to duck out on doing that stuff myself.

The list of things leaders must do is always long. Provided you are doing them, it's okay to dip into stuff you like to do, used to do, or simply can do. Consciously ensuring that you are spending the bulk of your time on the important things doesn't preclude serving others.

Whenever you're prioritizing—*or* delegating—remember: there is a balance to be struck within both.

PRODUCT? SERVICE? SEMANTICS

I REMEMBER A TIME when products were actual things—things you bought, things you held, tangible things with which you could *do* other things. I hear tell that you can still see them, even *obtain* them, in places like Lowe's and Best Buy.

But in tech especially, the line is blurred. Where software once was a product, we're being encouraged more and more to see software as a *service*. We don't go out and buy software these days; we download it from the internet (if at all) or subscribe to it and use it in the cloud.

I'm down with subscription-based services but feel the need to push back a bit on what I see as the diminishment of the notion of products, because I have an organization full of developers and the people from a plethora of disciplines who support them. And while the things they produce may, at the moment they become available for subscription, be seen by some as services, those developers knew what they were working on and that if they did their jobs well, what they produced would sell.

And when you create something that someone else wants and is willing to pay for, I couldn't care less what the term of the moment may be: you have a product. But in today's world, you should definitely offer it as a service. Just sayin'.

PRODUCTS, GOOD AND NOT SO GOOD

IF PRODUCTS ARE MEANT to address pains that those working in a given market or discipline face, is there a way to *rank* that pain? A scale—better yet, a test—of urgency?

There is indeed, and using it effectively is often the difference between products that people want and those that languish.

Before I explore this idea and add my own thoughts to it, I must credit the company that helped make identifying market pain a mantra for us, at SailPoint and before: Pragmatic Institute. (I strongly recommend the company to you.)

If you're selling a product intended to solve a problem—and every product is, right?—your odds of success rest upon three things: the *urgency* of the problem, the *pervasiveness* of it, and people's *willingness to pay* for your particular solution.

At SailPoint, my partner, Kevin, and I have boiled this down to what we have assigned the (unquestionably highbrow) moniker "the Advil/vitamin thing." (*See* "Marketing.") It goes like this: when a customer or end user has a pain point, but one that's just not very urgent compared to others, they might acknowledge it to a company (like ours) that comes along looking to develop solutions. "Yes," they might say, "that is an issue, no question about it. But it's only a priority C problem compared to these *other* things, which are priority A and B problems."

A lot of companies get in trouble because they don't hear (or choose to ignore) the second part. They develop products that address lower-priority challenges, then chase markets to sell them to. If they'd instead spent some time uncovering the *urgency* of the pain, they'd instantly get a pretty solid idea of the potential market for an effective solution.

I could leave it there, but I won't—because understanding the importance of developing products that are good and those that are just okay (or worse, not so good) is the cornerstone of building successful, lasting companies.

So you've identified the urgency of the problem. But before you run off to the designers and engineers, those two other tests remain: the problem's *pervasiveness* and the market's *willingness to pay* for an effective solution.

The fact that one or ten or a hundred people are experiencing urgent pain doesn't mean you have a business-building (let alone business-supporting) potential product. Thousands? Yes.

Don't get me wrong; niche products certainly have value. It's just that you're not going to build a large company around one. Which is not to say you should. There's nothing wrong with developing small companies that target niche problems for a set of people.

Let's say you build an incredible website about the history of the first twelve presidents of the United States. There will be some set of people (mostly in academia, I'd guess) who care—a *lot*—about that. But can you build a large private or public company around it?

Doubtful at best.

This is where the *scale* of urgency, mentioned at the beginning of this chapter, starts coming into focus.

There's *urgent*. There's *urgent and pervasive*. And then there's the trifecta: *urgent, pervasive, and money is no object*—er, *willing to pay*.

The advent of the internet has been wonderful in many ways, but before people figured out how to monetize it, it caused one of the biggest long-term stock market contractions in history.

Among the oldest (and truest) axioms of sales is that when you begin by giving product away, people will always expect to get it for free. The degree to which people with heads for sales had nothing to do with attempting to market the early internet is nowhere more clearly borne out than what was prioritized by its developers: it was all about eyeballs, right?

And for too long, Wall Street didn't even blink. But it wouldn't last—and without revenue, no product (or industry) can.

It's easy for people to sign up for something that's free, but over time, the internet got smarter about freemium models because it had to. So now, sites will often give *something* away—but not *every*thing. Everything is the premium version or the ad-free version, or whatever's on the other side of the paywall. You still need eyeballs, but by definition, a business *makes money*.

Facebook and Google figured it out, with two very different solutions to urgent, pervasive pains—respectively, communicating with friends and finding things easily in the needle-haystack world that is the internet. What's most impressive of all is that both did so despite their solutions not meeting the third criterion: having users who were willing to pay.

So they sold to advertisers instead.

To recap, (1) urgency: find pain, and make sure it's real and truly urgent by talking to the people experiencing it; (2) pervasiveness: Is it widespread enough to support a business? and (3) willingness to pay: Will the pain's sufferers—or someone else—pay for an effective solution?

PROSPECTS (VERSUS CUSTOMERS)

WHEN I WAS IN grade school, disruption was a bad thing. There was always that *one kid*.

"Timmy, you're being disruptive. Go to the principal's office."

Today, *disruption* has a whole new meaning and is overused to the point that I don't need to define it. But understanding what actually happens when markets are disrupted perfectly illustrates why existing companies must never stop chasing and listening to and developing products for prospects, while continuing to enhance the products and services their existing customers value.

I guess you could argue that this has always been true. Still, there was a time when business moved so slowly that companies could comfortably (and profitably) do what they did, day after day, year after year, for decades without changing much. But when we look at those companies now—those that still survive, and their numbers are dwindling—it's easy to see why hanging your hat on a particular profitable product is the same as inviting someone to turn your market upside down.

And not in a year or two, but a *month* or two.

Consider the changes roiling the so-called big three US automakers. Since the economic meltdown of 2007–2008, they have been profound. The resulting $80.7 billion government bailout of all three (it's a popular misconception that Ford got no government help) floated them through that crisis, only for them to meet a brand-new problem: ride sharing, which is on a path to make the economic crisis look like the good old days.

All three—in fact, all eleven—of the world's top automakers are promising to perfect driverless technology in the next few years, largely to compete with ride-sharing companies like Uber and Lyft. Those companies, in turn, have disrupted the taxi business in cities all over the world.

And, back to the automakers for a moment, I haven't even mentioned the move to electric vehicles.

Disruptions like these are the rule, not the exception.

If, like SailPoint, your company is more of the B2B persuasion, don't be lulled into thinking you won't face similar challenges simply because you are not dealing in consumer products. The ubiquity of technology has allowed the general knowledge of what companies offer to spread like never before, only increasing opportunities for disruption.

But there's a solution, and your sales force is calling on it every day of the week.

Disruptors tend to be people who talk to prospects—those who aren't buying the current offerings of existing companies—and who develop fresh ways to solve prospects' problems.

In other words, you're already getting the intelligence you need to stay nimble. The problem is you're not collecting and applying it.

That's because existing companies talk to their prospects from the perspective of what the company *already offers*. Their sales folks are so caught up in trying to convince prospects that their solution can work for them that they miss the prospect's complaint: "Yeah, but it could be so much *better!*" (For more depth on this, *see* "Markets, Listening To.")

And so the existing company is stuck, trapped in the logic of, "This is how we do this. This is how we've always done this. We've just got to make it better and better and better."

What they *should* be thinking is, "Wait. What if we just threw out that whole paradigm and came in with a new one that provides the answers our *prospects* are begging for?"

Your toughest prospects, not your existing customers, will almost always drive new product development, particularly of the disruptive kind.

But you have to be listening.

PUT YOUR MOUTH WHERE THEIR MONEY IS

VALUES ARE REAL.

They affect how people get hired, paid, and recognized.

How they treat each other at work.

At SailPoint, our HR team learned that when I talked with new hires about company values, it produced a very different reaction than just pointing folks to our values on the website (*see* "Four I's, The"). Something about being in the same room with the CEO of your new employer and hearing him or her say, "Look, this is how this works. This is why we're here. This is how we live it out," makes a difference.

I like to think there's an element of capturing the enthusiasm that new hires just naturally embody. They stand at one of the most exciting crossroads of life: a new start. Why not validate their choice to travel with your organization by showing you're with them all the way?

I like to think there's an element of capturing the enthusiasm that new hires just naturally embody. They stand at one of the most exciting crossroads of life: a new start.

Throughout the early stages of scaling up, my cofounder, Kevin, and I would do every new employee orientation. Now we usually have someone on the team provide the company and product overview kind of thing, but I still show up and really drive home the values piece. It's that important.

"At the end of the day," I'll sometimes say, "the difference you should feel at this company is that these values are not a plaque on the wall. They are how we live, how we work, how we measure and reward success and achievement. We aren't just saying these nice things. We're living them, and we expect every employee to live them too, because they exemplify, both inside and outside these walls, what SailPoint stands for."

It works. People regularly come to me and say, "You know, I've been here a year, and you're right. It's different here. What you said at orientation—that's really the way things are."

Some (okay, most) sound surprised. That speaks volumes about the promises some other companies have made and either reneged on or never even got close to, doesn't it? The same companies that churn through local labor pools and whose employees never seem to recruit their friends to the company as potential new hires. And the leaders of those companies don't even wonder why.

If I know nothing else, I know this much: there is incredible power in the boss standing up, looking new hires in the eye, and saying, "Look, what you're going to hear from me is *how* we do things. The *what* we do will continue to morph and expand. The how really won't, but by always expanding the what, we express our dedication to the first *I*, innovation. But if you keep focused on the *how*, we'll all get better and better and continue to build a great company."

RESEARCH

IF YOU'RE GOING TO go start a business, my general recommendation is to start it in a market you have some intuitive understanding of because you've spent some time in it yourself, whether it's high tech or mortgage banking or real estate—whatever.

That said, don't then adopt the stance that you know everything about it. You don't. (If you did, you probably wouldn't be reading this book. You'd already have your own book.)

People who fund businesses want research to back up your idea, and when it comes to research, there are two kinds: primary and secondary. (*See* "Markets, Listening To.")

You can read a lot about what's going on in an industry in trade journals, blogs, forums, whatever. It will help you understand industry pain and current solutions but in the most cursory way. All of that is secondary research.

If you're planning to start something in the B2B (or any other) realm, and all you have is secondary research, I have two words for you: *good luck*.

You have to talk to people who *live* the pain(s) of the industry in question; who can explicitly describe for you what their "day in the life" is like; and why their life's hard today, and most importantly, what would make it better. In our first company, my partners and I banged the phones ourselves, trying to reach potential buyers of the technology, and we used a market-research firm. We did it in the second start-up too, but not as much; by then we were pretty deep in the market ourselves.

The firm had great skill in getting people on the phone and keeping them on it, the stuff that we didn't have as much of because we're tech people, not market-research guys. What we did bring to the table was an understanding of the market's pain. We could pick up subtle clues about what people were frustrated with in their current products.

Over time, we developed an open question that proved powerful: "If we built a product that could do this, this, this, and this—how would you feel?"

And ultimately, we had an armload of responses like, "*Wow*, that would be great. That would be *far* better than what I have today." We knew that there was going to be at least some set of people who would have a lot of interest in that product. All we had to do was figure out how to make it.

Here's the asterisk: *do not* confuse people who say, "Oh yeah, if you built that, I'd buy it," with actual buyers, or, for that matter, investors. Potential customers—people who *say* they would *conceivably* buy a *product*—are not always the same people who will actually cut you a purchase order. And further, they are even less seldom the same people who will *buy in* to a company as an investor.

RUN TOWARD THE STORM

WHEN SAILPOINT WAS STILL young, we were aggressively courted by a very big name in technology.

We had fewer than one hundred people and were still venture backed. The due diligence process dragged on an entire quarter, but we got it done. Within a couple of weeks after the end of that quarter—Q2, as I recall—the paperwork was ready to sign.

But we had a little problem; we had missed the bookings target in Q2.

I was unsurprised. We'd never missed up to that point and did this time due largely to being driven to distraction by the due diligence that our large company friends had subjected us to.

You can guess what happened next.

Someone way up the chain at the company decided this was catastrophic and quashed the deal. Meanwhile, their team on the ground, the one that we'd worked so closely with, *still wanted to do it*. But this senior exec, despite having zero context, pulled the plug.

We'd tried to keep everything secret inside the company, but

But buffalo run toward the storm—because they intuitively know that's the quickest way to get through it.

when you're that small, it's hard. Probably a third to half of our people knew what was going on, and when it blew up, everybody was very sad. It is incredibly hard to go in and get back to work after a day like that.

Years before, someone had told me a story. I still don't know why or how it came back to me when it did, but the timing could not have been better. It was during a company-wide meeting shortly after we got this awful, awful news.

"You know, when a storm is moving across the High Plains," I began, "the wind comes up well ahead of it, often from the west. Cattle that are grazing stop and look up and then run east, away from the storm. Other animals hunker down as best they can. But buffalo run *toward* the storm—because they intuitively know that's the quickest way to get through it.

"There's a lesson here for us. We're facing down a storm, but now's not the time to run away from it. Nor should we freeze up and hunker down. We've gotta face it and run through it as quickly as we can, and if we do, we'll get through it a lot more quickly."

Now, years later, I still have people who were with us then who'll say, "That was a great story. I still tell it to my friends. And it's when I knew we were going to be okay."

We'd been kicked in the teeth. Everyone was really bummed and thinking, "Holy crap. We just missed our gold ring. We just missed our shot. A big company wanted to buy us, and we couldn't get it done."

But our folks responded. Their actions over the next days and weeks said, "No worries, Mark. We're on this. We're going to face this storm and run right through it." And we did.

And we're completely okay that big deal fell apart. Because we're worth almost ten times that amount today.

SHADES OF GRAY

PART OF A EVERY leader's job is managing their team's emotions.

One of the toughest things any of us does is (attempt to) view ourselves objectively, but as leaders, we have an obligation to do so. The reason? So we can understand how others view our words and actions.

The world is rarely black and white. Good leaders temper both ends of the spectrum because the extremes—good and bad—never last for long.

In the book's first chapter ("Authenticity"), I talk about the necessity of sharing good news and bad and trusting that, by treating people like adults, you win their trust. Corollary to that, however, is tempering news, both good *and* bad, to accurately attenuate it.

If you just had a bad quarter, it's important to add, "Hey—it's not the end of the world for us." If you don't *really have* catastrophic news, don't make it *sound* catastrophic. Conversely, you have to keep the successes in perspective; don't throw a party when your quarter is great.

The world is rarely black and white. Good leaders temper both ends of the spectrum because the extremes—good and bad—never last for long.

SHARED PAIN

WHEN WE FOUNDED SAILPOINT in early 2006, we took a relatively conservative amount of VC, because that's what you did back in those days with the dot-com bubble still in the rearview, albeit getting smaller every day. The only exceptions were longtime Silicon Valley companies, in which VC companies had complete faith.

That was fine with us. We were building products that we knew would be about twelve to eighteen months to get to market anyway, and sure enough, we launched in late 2007. By mid-2008, we probably had fewer than ten, maybe fifteen customers.

Then the mortgage crisis started to crack open.

Sequoia, one of the Valley's biggest VC firms, did a fifty-six-slide presentation titled "R.I.P. Good Times," and soon everybody was on the doom-and-gloom bandwagon. The gist was, "This is way worse than you think. This is nuclear winter. Cut deep. Cut hard. We're going to be in the doldrums for at least five years."

In the media more broadly, there was talk of another Great Depression, hard times the likes of which only the oldest senior citizens had ever seen.

So here we are, just coming off the ground. We have just a

handful of customers. Our VC board knew us; we'd worked with them at the last company, Waveset, and it turned out nicely—we sold to Sun Microsystems. Now they're almost three years into SailPoint, things are going fine—and BOOM.

They said, "You gotta cut. Do it to save cash. You gotta slash and burn." I think we had thirty or thirty-five people at that point, and they wanted us to cut a third. And I knew if we cut a third of the company, we'd kill it. We were a family at that stage. Everybody knew everybody. We'd all worked hard to get to market, and we did it together. And as leaders, we basically said, "With all due respect, no."

We did cut a couple of people who were on the performance border and took another guy from full time to contract. But everybody else in the company took a 10 percent pay cut.

We said, "That's as far we'll go, and we'll give people stock option grants to make up for the pay cut, but we're not cutting a big chunk of the company." It was the only time I've taken a very tough, not-doing-it stance with my venture team.

That's not the "right way" to go about it, if you subscribe to popular wisdom. You should take the pain and keep everybody else happy. But we decided, "Well, maybe that's true in general, but not for us." We were at such a critical point.

So we said, "We can't step on the gas and the brake at the same time. We're just accelerating out of our launch." We did hunker down, but we also got enough customers over the next three quarters to keep the bills paid. And from that point on, we grew and just never looked back.

It happened because we opted to share the pain, not inflict it on the people who got us to launch. And ultimately, the stock we gave our early teammates was way more valuable than the 10 percent they lost in salary in the short term.

Call me a hopeless optimist, but I believe that when you do the right things, everybody wins.

I love all the money people I've had the privilege to work with over the years, VC and PE. But there's a danger at the end of the day that comes with seeing things only through a spreadsheet. We're people, working hard to make other people's lives easier, better, whatever. Sharing pain allows us to do the same thing for each other.

TENSIONS (VERSUS PROBLEMS)

As a leader, one of the most valuable things you can do for your organization is differentiate between tensions your organization will always need to manage versus problems that need to be solved.

—*Andy Stanley*

THERE ARE ISSUES AT work and in all facets of our lives that cause us frustration. But not all of these issues are problems. When we come up against an issue and instantly decide it is a problem to solve, we risk short-circuiting what might in fact be an opportunity to make our companies healthier and more effective.

The key to distinguishing between the two types of issues— problems that need to be solved and tensions that need to be managed—is determining *whether* the issue can ever, realistically, be resolved or corrected. Or even *needs* to be.

If you're pretty sure it can't be solved, whether it's because you've already tried everything you can think of and nothing has worked or because you can't picture your organization remaining functional without this issue in place, you're almost certainly dealing not with a problem that must be solved but with a tension that must be managed.

Just figuring that out, in itself, is remarkably freeing.

If you realize that this thing is going to be with you no matter what, that it's a constant you must accept, you can develop strategies for managing it. You can get if not *comfortable* with it, at least *used* to it. You can accept it, learn its ins and outs and how it flows. What's the point, after all, in *fighting* what simply *is*?

Or maybe you decide it's a problem. Something you must resolve before you can move on. That, too, is crucial information, and again, frees you to act.

In the chapter "Balance, Life-Work," I talk about how we can never achieve a constant, perfect balance among all the facets of our lives. But if we can accept what I call *temporary healthy imbalances* and can train ourselves to cycle back to something *closer* to our ideal life-work balance after we've navigated these temporal circumstances, we will experience the sensation of our desired balance more often.

That is a working example, from our lives as a whole, of managing a tension. But what does that look like at work?

The first area that springs to mind for me is managing different types of people or groups in an organization.

For instance (and I'll admit to overgeneralizing here—somewhat), there are significant differences between managing creative types in a marketing department and accountants in the finance group. And between managing engineers and salespeople.

In the first example, there will always be tension between those who are motivated to deliver high-quality "artistic" content, such as graphic design, compelling photography, and other forms of messaging. However, much of the highest-quality content is also the most expensive—which tends not to sit well with the accounting team, which is charged with reining in expenses. So rather than see this as a solvable problem, I've found it better to understand and acknowledge that this tension exists and to manage it by ensuring that the leaders of both groups are managing the trade-offs optimally.

Or take the example of managing engineers and salespeople, which is pretty much standard fare in every B2B technology company.

Engineers want precision and excellence in their products and are sometimes guilty of believing that a product that is truly compelling will sell itself. Salespeople, on the other hand, fully understand that the actual "product" is only a part of the buying criteria that is under consideration in a business setting.

Salespeople know that prospective customers take into account numerous factors when making a purchase decision, from perceived ROI to ongoing support to industry peer acceptance. High-caliber salespeople therefore present the product as a key aspect of the overall solution but ensure that the "whole product," as it's sometimes referred to when incorporating all those other factors, is clearly differentiated in the minds of the customer.

Here again, reconciling these perspectives between teams isn't going to happen. So what's more logical and less stressful? Fighting reality—or accepting that periodic balancing and rebalancing of these opposing forces just comes with the turf?

As Andy Stanley's quote at the top of this chapter says, cultivating the ability to discern between tensions to be managed and problems to be solved is one of the most valuable things we, as leaders, can do. When we start to look at *every* issue we face with that discernment—at home, at work, in our communities—we take a giant step away from *reacting to* circumstances and toward *working with* them.

VALUES, *THEN* VISION

MANAGEMENT GURUS AND CONSULTANTS, even those claiming particular expertise in guiding start-ups, espouse mission, vision, and values, in that order, as the keys to a successful launch.

That might work for a handful of people who either set out to change the world or who wind up doing so as an outgrowth of their success. But based on everything I've seen, they're the exceptions, not the rule.

Steve Jobs had that kind of idealism and said as much: he preferred revolution to incremental change. That is nothing if not a vision-driven approach.

Bill Gates was less about revolutionizing technology and more interested in building a great computer company. That was his mission. Once he realized it, he became the world's biggest philanthropist. By any standard, that certainly constitutes changing the world. Still, his success was mission driven.

Maybe you believe with every fiber of your being that you'll be the next Jobs or Gates. If so, I wish you all the best. But the reality is that the huge majority of us are going to work in business areas that are natural extensions of what we've learned and really know, inside and out. That being the case, it makes a lot more sense to reverse the order of your priorities and define your company's *values* first.

Most of us who create new companies do so because we've learned a lot about a particular facet of business, and based on that knowledge, have come up with solutions to make it run better. While it isn't true for every B2B person I've ever met, a lot have spent five, ten, fifteen years getting intimate with a given arena and then go off and start a company to "build a better mousetrap."

Was that their vision all along? Their mission? In some cases, perhaps. In most, no.

A lot of direct-to-consumer companies are inspired to cure a pain that they themselves have experienced as end users. Consumer products is a mighty steep hill, and I have the greatest respect for those who reach the top (or even base camp).

In one respect, B2B is the same: you're trying to cure a particular pain that you have either experienced firsthand or that other companies you've worked with have pointed out—"You know, *this thing* is a real pain to deal with. Fix that, and you'll really have something."

> *The first thing I wondered was, "What kind of leader will I be?" My answer: "The kind of person I already am."*

So the gauntlet is thrown—and taken up, very often, by guys like my founders and me, who saw an opportunity and decided to tackle it (with a great team! *See* "Hiring"). *That* can be intimidating.

The first thing I wondered was, "What kind of leader will I be?"

My answer: "The kind of person I already am."

Knowing that and committing to it proved a literally bottomless source of strength and resilience for me, because I knew exactly what my values were and found it invigorating to think about basing a new company on those same values.

If your values are clear, you know what you care about. You know how you'll run your company and how you want to treat people. That will sustain you no matter what kind of business problem you're solving.

That's important, because the need for leaders to get their teams to pivot is only going to increase from here on out. You may start down one path, but because the feedback we can now access is so immediate and so much deeper, you shift—or at minimum, attenuate—your focus. If you get hung up on mission or vision, you'll be less willing to change your fundamental approach, even when it's clear to others that your vision is out of date or irrelevant.

Oracle was as successful when it shifted to creating applications as it was doing databases, though it never set out to be an applications company. Apple did not begin as a phone company. Neither did Nokia, which started with a single paper mill in 1865—and over its history, has been influential in forestry, rubber, cable, and (of course) electronics.

So if you're starting a company, invest some serious thought in how you want to run it. Define your values first. Because the why and where and what will likely change, but if your values are solid, your company will be too.

VALUING PEOPLE VERSUS CLAIMING TO

THE LAST OF SAILPOINT'S Four I's is "individuals."

"We value every person in our company."

I started working with a guy when he was in his late twenties, back at Tivoli. So I've probably known him for almost twenty-five years now.

In the first six months of Waveset, our last company, we were just barely off the ground, getting our arms around an enterprise product, and we didn't have a lot to show for it yet, and his dad got really sick in another state. And we just said, "You gotta go."

And this amazing guy is like, "Yeah, I know, but we don't have that many people right now. I can't. I'm on the team, I can't leave the team." And we were like, "Dude, you have to go."

We had twenty people or something. Maybe fifteen. But we just did the right thing. He'd been with us before, so we knew he wasn't going to flake off, knew he'd come back as soon as he could. We couldn't ask him to take a leave that would hamper us in keeping development rolling; we were running on VC fumes, and he'd have

"You can't say you value people but only do it when it's convenient or affordable. You have to put your money where your mouth is. All the time.

just said no. Sometimes you just have to insist.

It's one of those decisions that makes itself. There wasn't even any discussion about it. The leadership team members were like, "Of course! He's one of our guys. He's got to go do this thing for his family, and we'll support him, and he'll be back when he can. Sometimes this happens—and it can happen to any of us."

You can't say you value people but only do it when it's convenient or affordable. You have to put your money where your mouth is. All the time. This is probably the most important "walk the talk" principle in any business. Treat people the way you know you should, the way you'd like to be treated, and pretty soon, you have a culture people are telling their friends about. And that's when you know you've done the right thing.

VENTURE CAPITAL

INVESTORS, WHOMEVER YOURS ARE (or you're hoping they will be), must believe that you've identified a real market, one that is sizable with lots of bowling pins (*see* "Idea? Feature? Product?" Business?") and that the people in it will pay you for your product.

It's not enough that you believe in it. Trade places with your potential investors and ask what *you'd* want to know before pushing fat stacks of cash across the table (or at least wiring those stacks of cash into your account):

- *How big* is this thing you're tackling?

- Do you have the *skills and knowledge* to get this done?

- Are people going to *pay you a lot of money* for that?

- What's the *competitive* landscape?

Some early-stage companies will say, "Hey, look, I'm in this space, I found this really interesting niche, and the great news is there's *no competition!*"

Actually, that's terrible news.

It's highly unlikely that nobody else sees what you see. If something is truly a good idea, you are not the only one in the world who has figured out that it's a pain point or potential market. If such a promising market remains unmet, if others should be coming into it but if no one is, tread softly—there's usually a reason.

Understand, however, that this is very different from saying, "I'm still really early, and I have no significant competition already in the market." But if you're three years in? And there's still nobody else doing what you are? Potential investors and VC folks will say there's a reason nobody's doing it and move on, because the odds that some set of venture capitalists have already looked at this idea and rejected it are very high.

That said, VCs are not perfect. They've missed markets. They've rejected guys who later on built great companies. But a lack of competition (or potential competition, if the market is very new) isn't typically a validation point. Quite the opposite.

A friend who helped us with some of our early funding, Rob Adams, puts it more bluntly: "If I meet a guy in Austin who has what feels like a pretty good idea, I'll just tell him, 'Look, there are probably three guys in Seattle or New York and at least ten guys in the Valley already working on this.'"

Successful founders will largely agree—the closer you get to market, the more you find there's a bunch of other little firms out there doing something pretty similar to what you're doing. Again, this is good—it's validation. You've proven there's probably a market, because other people are chasing it too.

Now you have to differentiate by building a better team and better products and just flat-out executing better.

It's your investors' jobs to ask whether you can—and how you plan to.

WHEN KEY PEOPLE LEAVE

NO MATTER HOW GREAT you might think your culture is, it's like anything else: without regular maintenance, it can degrade.

In organizational terms, "maintenance" means checks and balances. Without them, practices that run counter to core values can manifest and become the new normal.

If you're serious about things like fairness and valuing your people and treating customers right and excellence (you *are*, aren't you?), there is no better way to ensure your core values are being upheld than by talking to key employees who've left to pursue other work options.

People leave their organizations for all kinds of reasons, so begin by embracing that truth. Somebody leaving doesn't necessarily mean they're fed up.

People leave their organizations for all kinds of reasons, so begin by embracing that truth. Somebody leaving doesn't necessarily mean they're fed up.

When a key person tells me, "Hey, I'm thinking about going," I say, "I just want to hear you talk about it. I want to make sure you're running to, not running from." It's a simple, short phrase that works. That's why managers use it.

Ultimately, it comes down to the last of the "Four I's."

We're working with individuals, and one individual's comfort with expressing discontent (let alone displeasure) with their work situation will differ from another's. (Shorter: Don't assume people will tell you when they're unhappy enough that they want to leave.)

Instead, take the opportunity that is presented to you when someone announces their impending departure. If they won't open up after you invite them to, encourage them further: "If something's not right here, let's figure out what it is and if there's anything we can do to fix it. But if you're just superattracted to the new thing and you tell me about it, and I say, 'Wow, you're right; that sounds really awesome!' you should probably go do it."

If that's what's happening—well, *fantastic*, right? Why would I want to hold them back?

"All I ask," I'll say (after congratulating them and assuring them they'll be missed), "is that you leave well."

In other words, if you're a senior person, don't walk in and think two weeks' notice is enough. Help us transition, and if your new company questions it, explain that it's the right thing to do—and that if and when you leave them, you'll extend them the same courtesy.

The only way we'd walk a senior person, a key player, out the door immediately is if they were going to a direct competitor—a desire that, I'm grateful to say, our culture at SailPoint seems to generally prevent.

Maybe it's because our folks just don't like the thought of working for a competitor. By far, the majority of key people who have moved on from SailPoint go on to do something else in the industry but almost never with a competitor and almost always with that thought of leaving well. I like to think it's because I tell them straight up, "Hey, this isn't the mafia. You won't be dead to me. If you leave well and you decide at some point you want to come back, we'll be here."

That's very different from some companies. You know the kind of organization I'm talking about: you're never supposed to leave, and if you do, you are dead to them.

We consciously establish very early on that working for us is not indentured servitude. We respect that you might actually come across a unique opportunity, or maybe more importantly, have a personal situation that demands you go in another direction. Just treat us with the same respect we've given you—the Golden Rule.

You let people leave. You encourage them to leave well. As long as they have, you welcome them back, if and when that day comes.

It's never easy to let key people leave, but how can I, a guy who left the security and certainty of an established company to do a start-up with friends, question others who might want to pursue that same path? Or want to leave just to pursue a different kind of path that they are convinced is right for them? As long as they're running to, not from, it's generally a good thing.

WHERE DOES IT HURT? AND HOW MUCH?

SEVERAL TIMES THROUGHOUT THIS book, I've referenced the importance of understanding market pain and of verifying *which* pains your particular market is clamoring for relief from. It's a concept I'm so enamored of that I've tried to reference it sparingly.

No more!

Market pain is really about market *research*, not selling. (*See* "Marketing.")

A prospective customer for your whatever it is says, "Sure, I like the concept of that."

"Great! Will you buy it?"

"Well—no, I'm not going to *actually buy it*, but I like the concept. I know people *like* me who would really like it, but it's not curing my *particular* pain.

"It turns out I have a headache," they go on, "and your vitamin sounds very interesting. But I gotta find some Advil. You're not Advil."

I can't stress it enough: find pain, make sure it's real, and *talk to*

I can't stress it enough: find pain, make sure it's real, and talk to people who actually have it.

people who actually have it.

Then verify how urgent the pain is, how many people have it (prevalence), and last but far from least, what it is *worth* to them—in *extremely specific*, absolutely monetary terms—to make that pain stop. (*See* "Products, Good and Not So Good.")

Once you have done all this—and assuming your whatever it is still looks promising—it's time to find some VC. (Which is always a challenge. Except in this book: it's under *V*.)

WRONG TIME FOR THE RED-EYE

BACK AT MY FIRST start-up, one of our sales guys had come from a big company. To his credit, he immediately got the message about frugality (on which I elaborate in the chapter "Shared Pain").

He just got it a little too well.

Like SailPoint, that start-up was based in Austin, but he was based in Houston and was then called to go see a customer up in the Northeast. So to save perhaps a few hundred dollars, he booked a three-hop red-eye. Needless to say, he wasn't at his absolute best for this critical prospect meeting.

When I saw the expense report, I was a bit stunned. The next time I saw him, we had a quick exchange that went something like this: "I really appreciate that you made the effort to be frugal," I began. I resisted the temptation to add, "But I really don't want you to be dumb about saving money when it involves being ready for a key customer opportunity." Of course, I was a lot more diplomatic.

A few years ago I was going to London and saw one of our other guys in the waiting area of the Austin airport. As we lined up to board, he was like, "Wait, what? You're in the same class as me?"

Austin to London is no short hop, but I take pride in being frugal when it makes sense. Business class? Sure. On a flight that long, those extra three inches of leg room loom large. But that's enough. I can skip first class for that one.

And that's the line between frugality and extravagance: knowing how much is enough. And if the situation warrants, sometimes that may mean choosing the option that isn't the absolute cheapest but is the most optimal for the need. So go ahead and take the direct flight for the key customer meeting. It's worth it.

XENOPHOBIA

xenophobia (noun) *xe·no·pho·bia* | \ ˌze-nə-ˈfō-bē-ə, ˌzē-\

*fear and hatred of strangers or foreigners or of anything that
is strange or foreign (Merriam-Webster.com)*

EVEN IF WORK NEVER takes you beyond the shores and borders of
your country, you're likely to collaborate with people from all over
the world. It doesn't matter what industry you're in, but it's also
accurate (anecdotally, at least) to think this is even more true in tech
than for, say, a midsized manufacturer in rural Indiana or Wisconsin.

If you're bringing into the workplace any preconceived notions
about groups or individuals being fundamentally evil or of them
"naturally" having "negative" ways of thinking, it's going to hurt you.
You'll miss opportunities to work with *great* people. You'll attribute
characteristics to people that are completely ludicrous and prejudiced
and not based in reality.

It's called *unconscious bias*, the notion that because we see one
aspect of a person or group, we put them in pigeonholes: "All (insert

an ethnic group or profession or political party or type of hobbyist here) are like *this*."

Of course, we most often hear about instances of this when *x* ethnic group or people from *y* country are marginalized, and it's wrong. But it happens based on those other aspects of life too.

For example, it's easy to think of rock guitarists as being a certain type of person, and looking at a photo of Tom Scholz, the guitarist of the rock group Boston, it's easy to imagine he fits that type:

Did you know Scholz earned a master's in engineering from MIT and was a senior product designer at Polaroid, back when he first began recording demos in his basement? Or that nearly everything on Boston's debut album, which at the time was the most successful debut record ever, was recorded in his home studio?

After Boston's initial success, Scholz founded a technology company that created music industry electronics under the trade name Rockman and sold the business to Dunlop Electronics. Today,

Scholz still tours as the last remaining original member of Boston and is an active philanthropist, supporting issues he cares about.

So if you're thinking, "All engineers or all salespeople or all service techs think (or are, or act) like *this*," think again. They *really don't*. Yes, they tend to come at their particular discipline from points of view many others within that discipline share, but *that's why you hired them*! To get a *global* picture—which only the full range of viewpoints can offer.

The same holds for the global *economy*: it takes all the parts to make up the whole, and only when each part is respected for its contributions can the whole potentially prove greater than the sum of its parts.

> *So if you're thinking, "All engineers or all salespeople or all service techs think (or are, or act) like this," think again. They really don't.*

YOU, THE CONDUCTOR

MY FAVORITE METAPHOR FOR leadership is that of the conductor of an orchestra.

Quite often, the conductor is someone who used to play a particular instrument in the orchestra, but now their job is to get the most beautiful sound out of the entire group.

You actually have a number of new jobs: selecting the music. Setting the tempo and the volume that you want various sections to meet. Sometimes you want more from the strings and less from the brass—and vice versa. And quite often, your job is to ensure you get the best quality from the totality of the group, because letting one soloist or one section dominate can ruin the performance.

You can't do any of this by grabbing the instrument out of someone's hand (particularly the one you used to play) and saying, "Let me show you how to do that." That musician won't want to play in your orchestra for long; nobody likes to be embarrassed, and nobody wants to be micromanaged. (And others still are highly effective when given free rein: *see* "Jazz.")

If you let sales or marketing or engineering dominate, pretty soon the people in your other sections (departments) will think,

Conductors don't actually produce music but draw the most from each section— from a collection of people— without ever producing a note.

"You know what—this guy only wants to play music where the horns dominate. I play strings. What's here for me?"

Conductors don't actually produce music but draw the most from each section—from a collection of people—without ever producing a note.

And they do it with their *backs* to the audience. Their focus is on the musicians and what they need them to do, knowing that if everyone does their job well, there will be plenty of applause at the end.

RECOMMENDED RESOURCES

Crossing the Chasm and *Inside the Tornado*, Geoffrey A. Moore

The Advantage and *The Ideal Team Player*, Patrick Lencioni

The Innovator's Dilemma, Clayton M. Christensen

Leadership Jazz, Max De Pree

The One Minute Manager, Kenneth Blanchard and Spencer Johnson

The Peacemaker, Ken Sande

The Peter Principle, Laurence J. Peter

StrengthsFinder 2.0, Tom Rath

StandOut, Marcus Buckingham

Up the Organization, Robert Townsend

ABOUT THE AUTHOR

MARK MCCLAIN is the CEO and founder of SailPoint (NYSE:SAIL), a leader in the enterprise identity management market. He has led the company from its beginnings in 2005 through its VC- and PE-backed stages to its IPO in 2017, as it grew from a team of 3 to over 1,200 employees and about 1,500 enterprise-class customers in thirty-five countries. He has been married for almost thirty-four years to his amazing wife, Marj, and has three incredibly cool adult children (Andy, Rachel, and Grace), three wonderful kids-in-law (Erika, John, and Pate), and four adorable grandkids (Melanie, Morgan, Malia, and Emmy) with two more (Levi and Lucy) on the way. He considers himself a very blessed person.